Getting Past Resistance
in Psychotherapy with the
Out-of-Control Adolescent

Getting Past Resistance in Psychotherapy with the Out-of-Control Adolescent

Vance R. Sherwood, Ph.D

JASON ARONSON INC.
Northvale, New Jersey
London

This book was set in 11 pt. Weiss by Alpha Graphics in Pittsfield, NH.

Copyright © 1998 by Jason Aronson Inc.

10 9 8 7 6 5 4 3 2 1

Library of Congress Cataloging-in-Publication Data

Sherwood, Vance R.
    Getting past resistance in psychotherapy with the out-of-control
adolescent / by Vance R. Sherwood.
        p.   cm.
    Includes bibliographical references and index.
    ISBN 0-7657-0149-9 (alk. paper)
    1. Adolescent psychology.   I. Title.
RJ503.S465   1998
616.89'14'0835—DC21   97-41460

Printed in the United States of America on acid-free paper. For information and catalog write to Jason Aronson Inc., 230 Livingston Street, Northvale, New Jersey 07647-1726. Or visit our website: http://www.aronson.com

In memory of my friend and mentor,
Charles P. Cohen, Ph.D.

CONTENTS

ACKNOWLEDGMENTS

Many of the ideas in this book were developed during my long association with the original Peninsula Village Residential Treatment Center. The long line of talented people who worked with me there all contributed to the experience that made this book possible. I include the line staff, nurses, physicians, program directors, and our first administrator, Laura Thomas.

I particularly want to express my gratitude to those who provided the clinical leadership when I was there: Larry Brown, Ph.D., Beverly Gibbons, Ph.D., Jim Lee, M.D., Nina Pennewell, Ph.D., Len Rudolph, L.C.S.W., and the Family Therapists: Jean Bolding, L.C.S.W., Kathy Pascoe, L.C.S.W., and especially Carla McCall, L.C.S.W.

I also thank the patients, who taught us everything.

INTRODUCTION

This book is a study of the out-of-control adolescent and, more particularly, the problems of trying to get treatment started with such a patient. We are all (far too) familiar with these youths. They are usually awful cases. They do not want to be in treatment, and they have been brought by parents who hope we can arrange some miracle that will arrest a long and steady deterioration in their child's functioning. The therapist has the patient delivered to the office and is asked to fix whatever is wrong. A nightmare follows. Matters are too far gone for the therapist to do much more than hang on as the patient continues his or her slide. The patient runs away, does drugs, shoplifts, is sexually promiscuous, threatens self-harm or actually makes suicidal gestures, has raging fights with the parents, or does any number of things that leave everyone associated with the case feeling perfectly impotent and furious. All of this is at its worst in outpatient settings, but even in hospital or residential treatment out-of-control patients can defy everyone's efforts at engaging them in a treatment process.

These are the patients with whom nothing seems to work. They can avoid whatever pressure we try to place on them through being out of control, that is, through being beyond parental—and thera-peutic—control. By contrast, most adolescent patients have lines they will not cross. No matter how angry, depressed, or rebellious they become, they stop short, for instance, of running away for days at a time, physically fighting with their parents, mutilating themselves, stealing the family car, or doing more than just experimenting with drugs. Or if they do any of these things, they don't keep on doing it. Most adolescents only flirt with moving decisively beyond parental control, even though they could, of course, do so at any time if they really wanted. Unhappily, however, there are those adolescents who are more than willing to cross that line and expose what all parents know but hope their children do not: that in this society it is quite possible for a youth to move far past parental control and come per-ilously close to activities that will fatally flaw or compromise the rest of the patient's life.

Roughly speaking, there are three ways such patients can be out of control. First, the patient's behavior may be out of control. Such be-havior may be confined to the family (such as damaging the family home or intimidating the parents in temper fits) or it may spill into the broader community. Behavior problems in the community may consist of statutory offenses, or offenses that are problematic only because the patient is a minor (e.g., truancy, running away from home or treatment centers, or underage drinking). Or behavior problems in the broader community may involve antisocial behavior—activi-ties that would be unacceptable at any age (e.g., shoplifting, drug dealing, or physical assault). By the time they get to the therapist's office most out-of-control youths will have a history of some sort of problematic behaviors and will be eligible for a Conduct Disorder diagnosis.

A second way that adolescents may be out of control is through drug and alcohol use. I am not referring to youths who experiment with drugs and alcohol or use such substances occasionally. Rather, I am referring to those patients who have developed or appear to be developing dependence on one or more drugs. The drug use clearly impinges on school and family. As drug use picks up, academics and participation in extracurricular activities slide and the patient becomes more and more withdrawn at home. In my experience it is almost unheard of for a patient to be heavily involved with drugs and not also have a history of problematic behaviors.

Third, adolescent patients may show mood and affect that are wildly unstable and out of control. These patients may be affectively quite volatile, and those living or working with them will observe wild mood swings. They may become terribly angry terribly fast, or they may become optimistic and euphoric so quickly that they launch into relationships and behaviors that are patently unpromising without even a glimpse of how slight are their prospects for success. Often these patients tend toward depression. They very often have surprisingly long histories of self-endangering behaviors, such as self-mutilation, suicidal gestures, or placing themselves in dangerous situations. Those for whom anger is more of a problem than depression may have assaulted their parents or teachers or found even worse ways to behave aggressively. Most patients who are affectively out of control also show behavior and drug problems.

How to approach such patients? Adolescents who have become out of control in these ways have declared independence from the adult world and feel that they have little to fear from the therapist, who nonetheless must make some attempt.

It is a mistake to focus on any of the above symptoms, on the ways the patient is out of control. These are not the true sources of resistance to treatment. Therapists who know how to study the case will find distinct, predictable patterns of organizing experience that underlie the overt symptoms. These patterns must be the target of therapy initially, and until they are engaged and mastered the patient will remain resistant to growing up. This book is a study of those patterns of resistance and of approaches therapists can use to bring those patterns under control.

To be sure, delinquent behavior, drug use, and affective instability can become so troublesome that something must be done to contain them; perhaps the patient will even have to be hospitalized or placed in a residential center. Even if the patient's out-of-control behaviors are temporarily brought under control, however, the patient will not be able to use treatment until the underlying resistance is handled.

The strategies and techniques described in this book for addressing the out-of-control patient's underlying resistance are intended, first, only for use with the out-of-control patient and, second, only for the resistance phase of treatment. The approaches I outline are unusual and unconventional, although they have, I think, solid theoretical foundations. These approaches are not intended for every case, nor for any but the initial stage of treatment. I want to emphasize this point: I am not suggesting a general treatment approach for all adolescents. Happily, most adolescent cases are not out of control, and it is not necessary to approach them in the ways detailed in the following chapters.

The first three chapters lay the theoretical foundation. The first chapter outlines the five underlying patterns of resistance I believe are evident in most out of control patients: narcissistic resistance, masochism, the paranoid stance, the schizoid defense, and affective lability. I present a brief sketch of each pattern and offer several clinical examples for each. The second chapter makes the argument that therapists must manipulate patients showing these patterns of resistance, that a direct, communicative approach cannot succeed. I make an argument for a more indirect, experiential style of therapy in these cases. The third chapter argues that all out-of-control adolescents show a particular type of narcissistic disturbance (not to be confused with the narcissistic style of resistance). This chapter seeks to outline just what out-of-control patients are resisting coming to terms with. I believe this narcissistic pathology is likely to dominate the rest of treatment, after the resistance stage has been (more or less) resolved.

The remaining five chapters address the five types of resistance. A completely different treatment approach is indicated for each. It is therefore important for therapists to be able to analyze what is happening and reach a correct conclusion about the patient's underlying pattern of experiencing the world. Only when the pattern is correctly identified can therapists understand what the patient is trying to accomplish and, just as important, what the patient is trying to avoid. With this knowledge the therapist can prepare interventions that have reasonable prospects of success. Otherwise therapists are likely to use the wrong approach. When this occurs, the therapist can actually solidify the patient's resistance; at best, the therapist's interventions will be irrelevant.

There are three remaining introductory points to be made. First, it is my experience that therapists seldom get the chance to see these cases through to their completion. It is more likely that a patient will have a succession of therapists, each of whom can contribute something to overcoming resistance and then to resolving the patient's deeper, narcissistic issues. Thus, failure with these cases is more the rule than success, although, of course, it is not really a failure if a therapist understands the case and contributes something toward ending the patient's resistance.

Second, the techniques I describe are, as already mentioned, unconventional. I do not intend this to be an invitation for therapists to be sloppy or freewheeling, however. I believe these cases call for a fairly accurate and detailed analysis and for interventions that are tightly aimed at what that analysis turns up. Even though I suggest unusual approaches, there is no place for a "shoot from the hip" style or for any treatment approach that is not built on a solid theoretical foundation. I must ask the reader, then, to study the second and third chapters, even though they are not as lively or interesting as the later, clinical chapters.

Finally, it is well not to think in too linear a manner with out-of-control patients. They do not show an initial resistance that is handled well, resolved, and gives way to a working stage of treatment, followed by termination. Patients may give up one type of resistance only to turn to another, and they may return to some form of resistance after a period of more honest work. I have seen very few out-of-control adolescents who moved steadily and cleanly through resistance, then to some sort of working phase, and then a clear termination phase. However, I do believe that therapists will not bring an out-of-control adolescent to a working phase—whether it is brief or long—until the initial resistance has been properly addressed.

CHAPTER I

FORMS OF RESISTANCE IN OUT-OF-CONTROL ADOLESCENTS

THE PROBLEM OF BEGINNING TREATMENT WITH ADOLESCENTS

Quite a bit of the literature on adolescent treatment has dealt with the opening stage, especially with the problem of getting the adolescent patient invested in therapy. The literature addressing this question is disproportionately large; it seems to me to be quite a bit larger, for instance, than the corresponding literature on forming a treatment alliance with adults. The reason for this is not hard to find; it may be discovered in almost any therapist's office. Indeed, those who have worked with many adolescents may feel that the problem of how to get a teenager invested in the treatment process has not been explored nearly enough.

Not only is the literature on beginning treatment with adolescents fairly large, it is also depressing. These patients pose unusual problems for the adults who work with them. At least part of the difficulty may be that the therapist's problems with the case do not come only from the patient's pathology. As Rinsley (1980) put it, even normal adolescents can baffle adults with "their emotional lability and unpredictability, the protean nature of their defenses, their bipolar swings of mood and thinking, their proneness to act out, their querulousness, fluctuant hostility, and preoccupation with their bodies and sexual feelings" (pp. 4–5). Indeed, didn't Anna Freud (1958) refer to adolescence as a period of "normal psychosis"? The therapist may have to battle not only the patient's pathology, but also the ways in which the patient resembles a healthy adolescent!

It is not surprising, then, that a multitude of modifications in technique have been proposed. These range from being authoritarian, to playing competitive games in sessions, to being overly permissive. Many modifications have been proposed for trying to approach delinquent and other types of out-of-control youth, and almost no one suggests that this population can be treated without some sort of modified technique. However, it is not only the delinquent patient who is a problem for therapists. There are many warnings in the literature that treatment with any adolescent will be difficult and perhaps flatly impossible. Gitelson (1948) thought it was a bad idea to try any type of analytically oriented treatment or one that probed very deeply, and others (e.g., Spiegel 1951, Eissler 1958) have noted how very difficult adolescent cases are. Fraiberg (1955) wrote that "almost all writers" acknowledge that adolescents typically have a negative initial response to treatment and that some sort of "special handling" is required.

I do not believe these writers are overestimating the difficulty of working with this population. Therapy with all but mildly disturbed adolescents requires the willingness and ability to work hard simply to get the patient into treatment. Just having the patient in the office or treatment center is scarcely enough. Months may be spent trying to establish some sort of interaction that will allow patient and therapist to speak more or less honestly to one another.

It is a little too simple, albeit correct, to say that the problem is one of resistance. All patients offer resistance, not just adolescents. Yet adolescent patients offer resistance that at least seems more difficult to influence. Therapists may even get the idea that there is not much more to the patient than resistance, that the resistance represents the entire personality (at least at that time), whereas adult resistance is almost always simply one feature among many present in the therapy hour. The adult patient is plainly made up of many parts, but the adolescent patient can seem to consist of resistance only.

Of course, this is not true. There is much more to teenaged patients than their efforts to avoid being known by the therapist, but it is hard to keep this in perspective. It is hard because adolescents in general lack perspective, and the way they communicate to therapists (and, so, to some extent the way the therapist experiences them) also lacks perspective. Except for those adolescents suffering relatively minor disturbances, this patient population cannot step back and reflect on what is going on. Far from reflecting, they give themselves to resisting in the same way they give themselves to most activities—it is all they are at that moment.

These considerations lead to a tenet for working with out-of-control adolescents, that the way to deal with resistance in out-of-control patients is to act as though there were nothing more to the patient than whatever form of resistance is visible at the time. Therapists must take the resistance seriously enough to focus on it exclusively. We may intellectually know that there is more to the patient and may even know what the patient is most likely to do next if the resistance is successfully addressed. However, since these patients lack perspective, they are swallowed up by whatever resistance they are showing at the time. If therapists forget this and try to appeal to the patient's good judgment, ability to anticipate consequences, or capacity to step back and reflect on what is going on, they will be ineffectual. The adolescent patient who is resisting is consumed by that task, and so therapists must attend entirely to the resistance—there is nothing else to the patient, at least not at the moment.

If one tenet for working with adolescent patients is that therapists must focus at first on resistance as though there were nothing else to the case, a second tenet is that adolescent resistance calls on the therapist to adopt interventions that are more experiential than communicative in nature. A communicative intervention aims to tell the patient *about* his or her life and is given by someone who is a little off to the side, occupying something of the position of a helpful commentator. Such a communication presupposes that the patient has some ability to let loose of resistance for a moment and consider or be impacted by the therapist's remark. By contrast, an experiential intervention aims to establish an interaction in which patients will have trouble maintaining the resistance with which they began the session.

This means *becoming a problem for the patient*. Therapy occurs when the therapist becomes a problem, the solving of which is incompatible with the patient's pathology (Cohen 1969). Therapy does not occur when the patient is creating problems for the therapist, which is what adolescent patients are especially good at doing. All modes of therapy, with the possible exception of behavior modification, try to pose problems for patients in one way or another. What I am suggesting is that the only reliable way to do this with adolescent patients is by manipulating the interaction so that the patient is maneuvered out of his or her preferred mode of resistance. Thus, the therapist relies on putting the patient in a position to *experience* an alternative to his or her resistance, rather than trying to *communicate* some content *about* the resistance. Each of this work's clinical sections will address some aspect of how this may be done.

A third tenet is implied in the second: the therapist should focus on the interaction with the patient rather than the patient's verbal productions or behavior. The important thing is the patient's impact on the therapist; this is what reveals the nature of the patient's resistance. In the early stages of treatment, the therapist's best source of information comes through interrogating his or her own feelings. These feelings may be understood in any of three ways, each of which may be accurate enough at one time or another. First, the therapist's feelings may be understood as instances of projective identification (e.g., Ogden 1982), or interactions in which the patient induces the therapist to experience split-off aspects of the patient's self. Second, the therapist's feelings may be understood as countertransference, or personalized reactions by the therapist that are in some way complementary to the patient's pathology.

Third—and this is the perspective most often relied on in this work—the therapist's feelings may be "pulled" by a patient's behavior and manner. In this case we may say that patients intend to establish an interaction with which they are comfortable, one that helps them avoid uncertainty and anxiety (Leary 1957). They therefore tend to behave in ways that maneuver the therapist into a role that allows them to maintain their preferred way of experiencing themselves. By pulling certain types of reaction from the therapist, they stay in patterns of behavior that keep them away from anxiety and change. Therapists may learn quite a bit about a patient, then, by trying to determine what the interaction is pulling from them. Interventions may then be planned by determining what sort of reaction is incompatible with the patient's preferred pattern of interaction. By interacting in a way that precludes the interaction the patient prefers, the therapist becomes a (potentially helpful) problem for the patient.

A final tenet is that therapists must do what the patient does not expect. The patient, after all, is working from a self–other paradigm in which the therapist is (in the patient's mind) assigned a certain role, one that is complementary to the patient's self-experience. If the therapist interacts in a way that is in keeping with this paradigm, resistance continues unchecked and the therapist simply accepts, as it were, the role given by the patient. The therapist must instead violate the patient's expectations (Cohen 1969). Whatever interventions the therapist offers should be aimed at disrupting the interaction the patient seeks. This is not to say that therapists should react crazily or at random; the clinical chapters in this work will focus on what responses will violate the patient's expectations and violate them in a potentially promising way.

THE FORM RESISTANCE TAKES IN OUT-OF-CONTROL ADOLESCENTS

Essentially this book is a study of the basic forms of resistance likely to be shown by out-of-control adolescents and the approaches that might move these patients toward something more adaptive. As may already be guessed, the concept of *resistance* is not used here to indicate specific behaviors patients use to undermine therapy. Rinsley (1980), for instance, has catalogued a number of such behaviors. These include the patient's adopting the stance of "buddy" or "pal" with the therapist (leveling), being flirtatious, taking an overly submissive posture, or being overtly rebellious. All of these are important forms of resistance, but resistance may be also understood in a broader sense.

The out-of-control adolescent primarily resists the therapist by living out of a self–other paradigm that makes it impossible to experience the therapist or hear interventions in a clean or undistorted manner. Presenting symptoms and forms of acting out are not nearly as important to the therapist as learning what sorts of paradigms the patient prefers or, more specifically, into what patterns of interaction the patient will try to force the therapist. No matter what particular behaviors the patient shows, the foundation of resistance will be the attempt to compress all interpersonal experience into an overly narrow, and therefore distorting, framework that supports the patient's sense of self and place in the world.

This means that resistance is not any specific thing the patient might say or do, or even a series of remarks or behaviors. It is, rather, the overall clinical picture during the therapy hour. Each session has a certain emotional atmosphere. The overall affective tone to the session is the therapist's first clue about what sort of interaction the patient is trying to create and therefore what pattern of resistance will be seen. This atmosphere is not something the patient establishes alone but is the result of an interaction with the therapist. No matter what are the patient's moods, behaviors, or verbal productions, the atmosphere that results depends on how the therapist is affected.

The session's emotional atmosphere in turn gives information about what role the patient wants the therapist to play. As noted, the patient is trying to engineer a particular pattern of interaction in which the patient plays one role and the therapist responds in a complementary fashion. Therapists can therefore note the emotional tone of the session and examine how that tone affects their experience of the patient. Therapists should assume that their experience of the patient is not haphazard but is instead at least partly the result of the patient's intentions. That is, therapists should start with the assumption that their experience of the patient reflects in some way the patient's self-experience. Once therapists gain insight into how the patient wants to be seen, they will be able to understand the exact form of resistance being shown.

This pattern during the therapy hour will usually parallel or complement the patient's behavior in daily life. This is not to say that the patient's behavior with the therapist will be the same as behavior at home. It may be the same—a defiant, belligerent adolescent may be verbally challenging and abusive with parents, teachers, police, as well as a therapist—but the patient may behave differently with the therapist, even though he or she is being influenced by the same self–other paradigm that led to treatment. A masochistic patient, for example, may be angry and volatile at home, idealizing and dependent with a date, and docile and seemingly open to help with the therapist. Over time it will become clear that all three patterns of interaction are designed to eventually pull rejection and sadism from the other person. In this example, the patient has adopted different ways of gradually accomplishing the same result; as each scenario with the parents, date, and therapist plays out, the patient will eventually feel degraded, rejected, and bound to the other emotionally. If, therefore, patients are different in sessions from what is reported at home or elsewhere, the therapist may assume that the different styles complement one another and that the patient's interaction with the therapist is headed in the same direction as interactions at home.

Most out-of-control adolescents can shift from one form of resistance to another over time. This may occur when the therapist has made a successful intervention, moving the patient out of one self–other paradigm into another. Patients may, however, move on their own in response to some change in their lives. When patients change in this way, the therapist should wait to see if the change endures or is brief. If the change endures, the therapist will have to change as well, matching interventions with whatever pattern of resistance the patient is showing (Eissler 1958). On the whole, however, there is continuity to the patient's resistance; generally the initial resistance is not exchanged until it has been successfully handled, and most changes in the patient's manner of interacting with the therapist are more apparent than real.

In summary, the therapist tries to understand the patient's resistance by focusing on the patient's overall pattern of interaction in the session. The patient resists by compressing the therapist's interventions into an overly narrow, pathological framework that distorts the communication, making it consistent with the patient's preferred self–other paradigm. The therapist may find additional information by comparing the patient's style in sessions with behavior outside sessions, working with the assumption that even different behaviors will complement each other in some way. Finally, even after the resistance has been understood, the patient may shift to a new pattern, which means that the therapist must shift as well.

BASIC FORMS OF RESISTANCE IN OUT-OF-CONTROL ADOLESCENTS

The five self–other paradigms most often seen in out-of-control adolescents are: narcissism, masochism, paranoia, the schizoid defense, and affective lability. The therapist may or may not be able to detect these paradigms from presenting symptoms. A patient might arrive for treatment with a history of heavy drug use, out-of-control behavior, and dramatic mood fluctuations and yet be operating out of any of these five positions. The symptom picture, therefore, will not necessarily tell the therapist what needs to be done with the patient, nor what the patient's mode of resistance will be. Indeed, the therapist will not know any of these things until it is clear which of the five paradigms the patient is presenting. Then the therapist can see in what way the patient is misinterpreting the situation and being duplicitous or dishonest.

Narcissistic Resistance

Adolescents who experience themselves in a narcissistic manner tend to come across as bored or indifferent during sessions. There is a constant implied judgment that the therapist is a waste of the patient's time; more aggressive narcissistic patients may be openly impatient, irritated, and disdainful. The therapist's experience of the session may be of being dismissed and struggling to maintain a sense of being potentially valuable to, or having meaning for, the other.

Narcissistic adolescents tend to appear self-sufficient and unconcerned. Not needing the therapist for anything, they can afford to be arrogant and to regard what the therapist might say with contempt. This contempt will sometimes be evident in sessions, but not always. Especially in an inpatient setting, narcissistic adolescents may be compliant and agreeable during individual sessions only to resume a more openly scornful, independent stance after leaving the therapist. In this case, the patient will hold the therapist in particularly strong contempt since the patient will feel that he or she has successfully fooled the therapist.

Whatever the therapist says to the patient will be filtered through the illusion of self-sufficiency and grandiosity. Therapists may try to point out the obvious, that the patient's approach to life is not working very well or that the patient has some fairly evident problems. The patient will not hear this intervention accurately. As Miller (1986) has pointed out, a patient must be thinking realistically to learn from experience or from an observation about his or her experience. Narcissistic adolescents are certainly not thinking realistically, however, since everything is being heard through the illusion of self-sufficiency. These patients will assume that the therapist has made the remark out of envy of the patient's freedom, because the therapist is paid to say such things, or because the therapist, like all adults, does not want the adolescent to share adult riches and prerogatives. Consequently, no matter what the patient says, he or she has already dismissed the therapist's confrontation.

The therapist may come to feel toyed with after a time, aware vaguely that the patient is playing games—to the extent there is any involvement at all. Often therapists simply become more shrill or aggressive in their approach, understandably frustrated that there seems no way past the patient's unrealistic but unyielding grandiosity. Unhappily, any expression of weakness on the therapist's part (and becoming more aggressive will be seen, correctly, by the patient as weakness) only feeds the patient's narcissism. These patients are competitive in their approach to life, and they feel inflated when they best someone. The patient feels more confident and safe as the therapist feels more stymied.

A 14-year-old girl came to treatment after several brushes with the legal system. Her father clearly worshiped her and had spent the previous two years bailing her out of trouble. By the time he reluctantly brought her to treatment under pressure from juvenile court, the girl steadfastly believed there were no consequences to her behavior. She felt someone would save her from whatever might come up. Her private explanation for this circumstance was that no one would resist or deny her. She responded with arrogant disdain to anyone who suggested otherwise. Occasionally in therapy she would seem a little engaged, arguing briefly with some point her therapist made. Most of the time, though, she was plainly indifferent to what was happening in sessions. She very clearly felt bulletproof.

A 15-year-old girl in her first session came across as bright, inquisitive, and oddly challenging. The therapist found himself liking her quite a bit and wondering why. He realized in the second session that the patient was extending a silent invitation to him: if he would see her as special and take her side against her mother, she would in turn idealize him. In the third session, he was challenged by the patient in a way that made it necessary to set a firm limit with her. As soon as he did this, all pretense of affiliation disappeared; the patient began to denigrate the therapist and then flew into a rage, eventually throwing a lamp at him.

A 15-year-old boy was charming and engaging with his therapist. His mother had brought him for treatment after she learned that he was "into drugs." In fact he was selling marijuana and using several other drugs. He was also missing quite a bit of school, stealing money from his mother, and shoplifting. He regularly manipulated his mother, who could just barely bring herself to believe that her son was involved in any problematic activities. The patient assumed he could manipulate the therapist too and offered himself as an engaging, likable, bright young man. When the therapist was not charmed, he became scornful, aloof, and indifferent in sessions, usually refusing to talk at all. Between sessions he tried to persuade his mother that the therapist did not know what he was doing.

Before moving to the next form of resistance, we should study what I believe is a special case that falls under the heading of narcissism, namely, those patients who suffered severe forms of Attention Deficit Hyperactivity Disorder (ADHD) as children and began to show bipolar symptoms during adolescence. These adolescents typically retain many of their ADHD symptoms, but there are two changes in the clinical picture. First, psychostimulants stop having a therapeutic effect and, second, these patients become increasingly short-tempered and aggressive as puberty continues. While they do not show all of the symptoms of a classic manic episode, they do frequently respond to lithium, and so there is justification for regarding the clinical picture as an Atypical Bipolar Disorder (Biederman 1997, McElroy et al. 1997).

Even though the origin of these patients' pathology is apparently biological, I include them here because their interpersonal manner is essentially narcissistic. They tend to be detached from others and not to develop lasting relationships with peers. They are not exactly indifferent—they are in fact highly reactive to others. However, their reactions are just that, re-actions; they are stimulated by other people, but their responses do not indicate affiliation or connectedness. Rather, others are primarily sources of excitement and stimulation.

In sessions, these patients tend to be hostile and irritable. They are usually angry to be in treatment, an engagement they find boring and therefore aggravating. They are no more involved with the therapist than are other narcissistic adolescents, and they are more inclined to express their lack of involvement by being late or missing appointments. They tend to be remarkably egocentric and incapable of reflection.

The therapist's experience with these patients is that of trying to flag down a passing car. The patient's self-centeredness, lack of interest, and frequent hostility leave the therapist with no reliable avenues of approach. Even if the patient is depressed or upset during a session and seems to become a little more dependent on the therapist than usual, this is not likely to last until the next session. In general the therapist is an annoyance to this type of patient, who makes sure the therapist knows it.

A 17-year-old male with a long history of learning disabilities and ADHD-related problems was referred for treatment after he refused to attend school any longer, saying there was really nothing he needed to learn. His parents and therapist suspected he was afraid that he could not pass and would not graduate with his class, but the patient showed no hint of this, nor would he acknowledge it when confronted. He came and went at home as he pleased, began to use marijuana heavily, and plainly felt entitled to whatever he wanted. He was angry to the point of being assaultive with his parents and had numerous fights with peers. He started to live on the streets, saying he found the freedom of that life to be "a real high." In sessions he was openly scornful of an adult world that, he said, had nothing he wanted. Usually he would not even respond to the therapist's interventions. His chief production in therapy was to complain of boredom and to engage in long, angry speeches about the follies of the adult world. He fidgeted throughout sessions and talked in a rapid, pressured way. As a child the patient had been on Ritalin and it was tried again, but the medication had lost its paradoxical effect, making the patient even more excited and restless. Eventually he was placed on lithium, which controlled most of his restlessness and excitability and helped him become less hostile.

Masochism

At first glance, masochistic adolescents may seem treatable. In early sessions they often parade their problems and weaknesses in a docile manner, apparently asking for help and offering little resistance. Clinically these patients seem depressed, and the fact that they are apparently in pain gives the therapist the illusion of being helpful or needed. There is a kind of submissiveness to their interactions; it is easy for a therapist to mistake this for compliance or even gratitude.

Matters are not, however, what they seem with masochistic adolescents. If the therapist initially believes the patient to be allied, doubts soon begin to arise. For one thing, the therapist may note in the patient's history a disturbing number of self-endangering behaviors. These patients, who tend to be female, typically have been physically abused by boyfriends or raped. At the very least, the patient is repeatedly taken advantage of by friends. Such a history may lead the therapist to wonder if it is the patient's intention to be degraded and, if so, whether the patient will let the therapist be of help.

Masochistic adolescents invite the therapist to make helpful suggestions about what would solve their problems. Patients who do not make such an invitation directly frequently tell of a painful event and then wait passively. The therapist may feel somehow pressed by the patient's passivity to offer a solution or idea. If, however, a solution is proposed, the therapist will find it was not helpful. The patient will either reject it out of hand or will try it out, only to report that it did not work. Soon the therapist may begin to feel irritated or even provoked.

The therapist's experience of the patient is an excellent indicator of whether a patient is behaving in a masochistic manner. In a word, masochism breeds sadism. Therapists will eventually feel drawn to attack masochistic patients, and they may find themselves wanting to make abrasive remarks, offer gloomy (somewhat punitive) prognoses, or even cancel sessions. The therapist's own growing frustration and irritation parallel what the patient does to most persons, namely, elicit attack (or at best indifference). When therapists find themselves angry and punitive toward a patient who formerly seemed docile and open to help, it is usually a sign that the patient is masochistic.

Even if the therapist confronts the patient with what is happening, matters will not change. Adolescents who interact along a sado-masochistic axis typically do not leave that pattern for long, no matter what the therapist says, interprets, or otherwise points out. Often the intervention itself will be heard by the patient as a rebuke or attack, leading the patient to become even more submissive, weak, and seemingly hurt. Unable to get through, therapists may find themselves wanting to attack all over again or, perhaps, feeling guilty as a reaction formation to their growing anger. Even the most patient therapist will likely feel impatient and irritated by masochistic adolescents.

A nearly 18-year-old girl was brought to therapy by her parents. She had a long history of being taken advantage of by boyfriends and friends alike. She bought things for those around her, gave gifts, and did favors. These maneuvers did not win friends, unfortunately, but always seemed to leave her on the outside. Her friends took her gifts and favors, and her boyfriends used her sexually, but no lasting relationships ensued. Her parents had always been worried about these patterns, but they grew alarmed and sought help when she was physically roughed up by a boyfriend. In sessions the patient tended to smile weakly and resembled nothing so much as a young dog bearing its throat to an older, more dangerous animal. She seemed not to comprehend much of what the therapist said, even though it was not complicated, and she looked injured by what she did understand. She often looked hurt and depressed by the end of a session. Over time, the therapist came to dread sessions, had trouble staying awake, and found himself occasionally making derogatory remarks. Eventually the therapist suggested hospitalizing the patient. While there were some clinical reasons for this, the therapist admitted to a colleague he feared he was simply trying to punish the patient.

A 17-year-old girl was brought to her fourth outpatient treatment by her mother. She initially impressed the therapist as bitter and depressed and as being a defiant young woman. Even though her angry rebellion never fully dropped away, the therapist began to sense that the patient was more masochistic than defiant. It turned out that she had been raped seven times and had been physically beaten by boyfriends on multiple occasions. Although the patient did not, like most masochistic adolescents, openly parade her weaknesses, she nonetheless managed to reveal herself as inept and helpless, eventually drawing some sort of attack from most of those around her.

A 14-year-old boy came to treatment with a docile and submissive attitude. He initially won a sympathetic response from the therapist, telling of the many times he was beaten up, stolen from, and made to perform various degrading favors for the older boys in the boarding schools he had attended. However, the therapist began to wonder why this young man never stood up for himself and whether those who took advantage of him had been subtly invited to do so. The therapist initially found himself wanting to help this patient and extended himself to do so, but he quickly tired of the effort. Whenever he offered help or suggestions, the patient found some way to sabotage the situation. The patient would forget to follow a plan, fail to accomplish an agreed-upon task, or simply mutter helplessly that he had "screwed up" the strategy he and the therapist created. After a time, and to his surprise, the therapist began to feel more sympathy with those who had taken advantage of the patient than with the patient himself.

Paranoia

It is rare to find an adolescent who is firmly entrenched in what would be called paranoia in an adult. However, there are patterns of experiencing the world that are decidedly paranoid in nature; while these may not result in a full-blown paranoid picture, the dynamics are substantially paranoid, and we may use that term to describe them. In essence, paranoid adolescents are those whose interactions are built around mistrust, cynicism, bitterness, and anger. These include many of the overtly defiant, delinquent, conduct-disordered youth so familiar and frustrating to mental health professionals. They accuse others of intending some unfair treatment and then use the suspected injustice as an excuse for their own deviant behavior.

Most therapists can recognize that they are being challenged and provoked by such patients, or that they would be if they pressed the patient at all. They sense the power struggles these individuals seek to create, and they wisely try to avoid them. This, however, is much easier said than done. Mistrustful adolescents have already defined the therapist, and almost every other adult, as something of a police officer, intent on controlling and dominating the patient. Whatever the actual intervention, the patient will respond as if the therapist had tried to coerce submission. Often the patient can elicit the power struggle the therapist had consciously sought to avoid.

The therapist's experience of the case depends in part on his or her own inclinations and, perhaps, pathology. Those with their own unresolved rebellious streaks may identify with the patient and try to show that they are kindred spirits. More compulsive therapists may enter into a power struggle, trying to show the patient who is boss. Narcissistic therapists may feel irritated and increasingly bored or indifferent, eventually preferring to work with the parents, who are more appreciative. Of course, all of these responses leave the patient's paranoid style intact.

> A slightly manic, 17-year-old drug addict was much drawn to life as a beach bum. He would leave his parents' comfortable, upper-middle-class home and live with friends on the beach for weeks at a time, imagining that he was showing his disdain for "the Man" and for a life of obeying societal convention. He was excited by the prospect of not being at society's beck and call, of being free and deviant. When his family succeeded in bringing him for therapy sessions he was obnoxious and provocative. He let it be known that he regarded the therapist as an extension of his parents and declared that all the therapist really wanted was to make him "wear a suit!" No matter what the therapist said, this young man heard it as a demand for conformity or for giving in.

> A 16-year-old girl had very early formed the view that her parents were frauds. She felt they simply wanted to show that they had power over her, and she went to great lengths to show that they did not. She dropped out of school, used drugs heavily, became pregnant without knowing who the father was, and otherwise adopted an unconventional lifestyle. In a succession of treatments she regarded her therapists warily, sure they were simply intent on making her "kiss ass." She was intent on not allowing herself to depend on a therapist, certain that any attitude of submission on her part would result in being taken advantage of in some way. She was angry, accusing, and perpetually challenging in sessions.

The Schizoid Defense

Even though many schizoid adolescents have histories of antisocial behavior, including violence, in sessions they tend to be quiet and remote. The word that is most often used to describe these adolescents is *passive*. While there may be a hint of irritation from time to time, for the most part these patients go through sessions like a prisoner doing time. They seem resigned to a fate they would rather have avoided.

At times these patients will seem to touch on something that sounds important. However, it will not go very far. If the therapist seems interested and pursues the topic, the patient scurries away, changing subjects or simply becoming mute. Even if the therapist does not pursue the topic, it will go no further. The patient in either case will find a way to touch the issue and then leave it, a pattern repeated in relationships.

The therapist will realize after a time that the patient mostly wants to be left alone. Even the patient's pattern of drug use (in my experience, most such patients are drug users) is unusual in this respect: while most adolescents use drugs with peers, schizoid patients usually use drugs alone. After a time the therapist realizes that these patients are in fact always alone, no matter where they are. The therapist realizes this after finding that he or she feels alone even while the patient is in the room.

The therapist's efforts to make contact are usually defeated by the patient's ability to be passive and resigned. Verbal interventions are usually tuned out; if they have an impact, the therapist will not know it. If the therapist asks whether there is anything at all the patient wants from the therapist, the answer will often be a quiet and thoughtful no.

The schizoid adolescent's manner simply negates the therapist and precludes the possibility of a connection between the two. The therapist is left with no good way to make contact. The patient is not usually rude or obnoxious, as with narcissistic adolescents, but is simply uninvolved. There is a wall around the patient, and there is really no way to penetrate it or gain access to the patient's inner world.

A 16-year-old boy had been in three outpatient treatments. He stayed away from his family almost entirely, living alone in his room, mostly smoking marijuana and listening to music. He had not been successful in making friends or fitting into an exclusivistic peer culture after his family moved to a new town. He had tried to hang out with his older sister and her friends but was discouraged from this by the sister's irritation. He accepted defeat and decided to be alone. Over a two-year period he isolated himself almost completely. When pressed by his parents he would sometimes become enraged to the point that his mother was afraid of him. He said, and seemed to mean, that he wanted only to be left alone. Therapists who worked with this patient found it hard to get anything meaningful from him. He would exchange small talk but when pressed to go deeper would only say that he wanted to turn 18 and leave home. He said there were no problems he wanted to work out and was simply biding his time until he could leave. He said he had no problems and was "okay" with his current life. He was flat, uncommunicative for the most part, and indifferent in sessions. Therapists tended to like him but never felt any real relationship forming.

Affective Lability

Affective lability is the one form of resistance the therapist may have to deduce from the patient's history and life outside sessions rather than observe directly. Affectively labile patients come to treatment with histories of mood instability; they have frequently made suicidal gestures, placed themselves in dangerous circumstances, and/or mutilated themselves. Mood instability seems associated in these patients with dating relationships or, less frequently, with close friendships. Most suicide attempts and other self-endangering acts take place in the context of losing someone. On the other hand, entering into a (seemingly) close relationship can make these patients feel something approaching euphoria.

Most of this goes on outside the therapy hour, so it is hard for the therapist to have direct evidence. It is unusual for these patients to seize on the therapist as someone to whom they might become closely attached. In therapy sessions these patients tend to be uninvolved. They treat sessions like a duty or task to be finished, much like going to school. They are not personally involved in sessions, and they certainly are not invested. Consequently, the therapist has little leverage and no sure means of knowing what is really going on in the patient's life. The first clue is usually a report from the family that the patient has done something dangerous.

The patient is trying, in essence, to avoid competence (cf. Kroll 1988). These are individuals who do not want to be alone or emotionally separate. They feel at ease only when attached to someone else, and the attachment must be such that they can feel relieved of the burden of individuality. For such patients, attachment is based entirely on need. Their fear, therefore, is that any sign of competence, growth, or independence on their part will be taken as evidence by the other person that he or she is no longer needed. They fear that the other person, not feeling needed any longer, will retaliate by moving on. Consequently, the relationship might end if the patient takes any steps toward competence. When faced with loss of a relationship, these patients often hurt themselves as a way of coercing others to resume closeness.

Therapists may catch some glimpse of these dynamics in sessions if the patient is especially depressed and looks to the therapist for relief. The problem for the therapist is essentially the problem with needy, angry, adult borderline patients: the patient defines relatedness in terms of need satisfaction or tension relief; if the therapist cannot offer relief when the patient seeks it, the patient will either feel rejected or assume that the therapist deliberately withheld help. In either case, the therapist is left with no good means of communicating the possibility of a different sort of relationship, one not built on tension reduction.

In this case, the patient will distort virtually any communication from the therapist. The patient, feeling in the midst of a crisis, will not be able to hear the therapist say that he or she sees the situation differently or that the therapist thinks that what is needed is working the crisis through rather than seeking relief from it. Any such intervention, even if accompanied by empathy and understanding, will be heard by the patient as some variety of abandonment. The therapist will have the sense that "I'm not getting through," or perhaps of having been dismissed as a disappointment. The patient seems ready, at least occasionally, to see the therapist as an omnipotent caregiver but seems to have no tolerance for anything less gratifying.

A 16-year-old boy had been a recluse and a loner for many years after finding he could not make friends easily. He feared that reaching out to anyone would make him so hungry for a relationship that he could not stand it. He lived a depressed, fantasy-ridden existence, chiefly thinking about living by himself in a forest, far away from civilization. When he started treatment, the therapist suggested that the patient try to make a friend to see what would happen. The patient needed only the one suggestion and quickly latched onto an admired peer, seeking to be his constant companion. Initially, the patient was enthused and enlivened by his contacts with this peer but quickly came to fear that the relationship was doomed to end eventually. Even though no end was in sight, the patient became bitter and angry, in part at the therapist for "getting me into this!" After only two weeks, the patient decided the relationship was doomed (although there was no evidence of this) and mutilated himself by gouging at his wrists with a sharp, pointed object. The next week he made a fairly serious suicide attempt by slashing his wrists with a razor. The therapist wondered what had happened; in the course of less than one month the patient had gone from a depressed and withdrawn state to elation and euphoria and then quickly to a self-destructive state of mind. The therapist felt that he was somehow being attacked and punished (the patient later confirmed this) but was not sure what for.

A nearly 18-year-old girl was brought to therapy by her parents, who described a series of dangerous car accidents. The girl was desperately involved in an intense, chaotic, and definitely unstable dating relationship. The therapist thought the accidents paralleled periods of distress in that relationship. It turned out that the patient could not tolerate being without a boyfriend for more than a day or two. Whenever she felt unattached, she became grossly depressed, desperate, and passively self-destructive. She seemed to have no ability to step back from the chaos she felt in sessions and reflect. Any attempt on the therapist's part to point out patterns, suggest alternatives, or confront obvious distortions was met with silence and withdrawal. The therapist felt utterly ineffective and irrelevant and strongly suspected this was also what the patient felt.

CONCLUDING THOUGHTS ON
ADOLESCENT RESISTANCE

I have chosen to categorize adolescent resistance in terms of broad types of psychopathology rather than in terms of developmental issues. It may be possible, with mildly disturbed adolescents, to think cases through in terms of developmental tasks gone awry or become problematic. It has not been my experience that this is especially helpful, however, with out-of-control youths (this issue is discussed further in the next chapter). Age-appropriate issues may come to dominate the middle or later stages of therapy, but this is not what the therapist will see at first. Rather, the therapist will see a broad style, or pattern of interaction, that colors the session. The patient is avoiding age-appropriate tasks through these patterns of interaction and, until they are addressed, any developmental issues will be hidden from the patient's sight as well as from the therapist's interventions.

Each of the five types of resistance described earlier could also, in an adult, be regarded as a personality type. Indeed, it may appear that these are simply different forms of personality-level psychopathology labeled as resistance. If we were discussing adults, such would be the case. However, the appearance of, for example, pathological narcissism in an adolescent does not mean the same thing it would mean in an adult. In an adult, pathological narcissism defines the patient; it is the patient's identity, or it is at least the style in which identity expresses itself. By contrast, the adolescent's identity is still fluid.

We may think the matter through by applying the category of *commitment*. Identity is one's (conscious and unconscious, deliberate and accidental) commitments (Sherwood and Cohen 1994), whether this is as mundane as being committed to working in order to care for one's family or as high-minded as being committed to a value, such as pacifism. Adolescents do not have the staying power to let us speak of such commitments. The process of being committed is the process that creates identity, and the strength with which commitments are held is what we mean when we say that an individual is strong (or weak). An adult can be committed to a paranoid view of the world, for example, and to paranoid ways of experiencing self and other. An adolescent, by contrast, may *prefer* such an experience and may cling to it because it allows escape from anxiety. However, the adolescent can usually be induced to give up that experience, whereas an adult may never completely surrender it.

The rest of this study is given to describing how therapists may recognize the pattern of resistance a patient shows and what strategies may be used to defeat the pattern and move to something that allows a more honest and promising interaction.

CHAPTER 2

THE ROLE OF MANIPULATION IN THE TREATMENT OF OUT-OF-CONTROL PATIENTS

THE QUESTION OF MANIPULATION

The most important factor in the early stages of therapy with out-of-control adolescents is that the patient does not want to be there. It is unusual to work with an adult patient who is in this position; there are only a few circumstances that place an adult in a therapist's office against his or her own wishes. The reverse is true with deeply troubled adolescents—there are few circumstances that place them gladly in a therapy session. Even a reluctant adult has at least some motivation for therapy to succeed, but adolescents can throw their full weight into defeating the therapist.

The tenacity of adolescent resistance is hardly surprising. Even a healthy adolescent hardly knows how to be honest and self-disclosing at the same time; that presupposes considerably more integration and integrity than a personality under construction is likely to have. In addition, interactions with an adolescent will be skewed by the fact that it is a parent surrogate the adolescent is having to deal with in therapy; even normal adolescence is, after all, a time of life when interactions with adults are strongly colored by the youth's desire to get away from the parents and the nearly as strong desire not to get away at all. Finally, but not at all insignificantly, adolescents do not want to be understood. Anyone with an unstable sense of self experiences being understood as the equivalent of being emptied out or possessed by someone else. Being known by an adult can therefore be threatening to an adolescent, and communications with the therapist will be colored by the desire to remain a mystery in order to safeguard the sense of self.

If these things are true of relatively healthy adolescents, those who are seriously troubled may be expected to put up even more barriers. Therapists are naive if they believe most adolescent patients are capable of being real or genuine in the opening stage of treatment or that these patients will gradually respond if the therapist just shows good technique. By contrast, the therapist will quickly be aware that there is considerable dishonesty, duplicity, and manipulation involved.

If it is to be a successful treatment, there must be some manipulation on both sides. It is a given that there will be some of it—quite a bit of it, actually—on the patient's side. But the patient should not be the only one who is willing to be manipulative. A key theme of this book is that the therapist must be willing to manipulate the patient into beginning to abandon pathological interactions and their corresponding self and object images. I say *manipulate* because the therapist cannot accomplish this goal directly. A direct communication to someone who is not able to be honest will be distorted in the interest of the hearer's dishonesty or, in this case, pathology.

For one example among many, a rebellious, defiant adolescent will feel most comfortable when adults are experienced as police, as if their intent were to control and dominate. Such youths will interact in a manner that allows them to experience adults in precisely this way. In many cases, these youth are able to bring just such an interaction about, gradually coercing their therapists, at least briefly, into the role of lawgiver, rule enforcer, or judge. Even if therapists consciously resist the role, the patient will likely experience them as if they had not. There is no nonmanipulative way to get around this distortion and therefore no direct way to speak to this patient and be heard. There are, however, ways to manipulate the patient into a very different experience of the therapist; when this is done, the patient may be spoken to more directly.

The word *manipulation* may sound distasteful to therapists. Many of us are none too comfortable with our latent psychopathy, ruthlessness, or aggressiveness, or we fear we might easily become far too comfortable with such things and struggle therefore to keep them under control. Manipulation travels too close to these unwanted elements of human life, threatening to revive infantile omnipotence with the sense that we are above the rules after all and can toy with other persons like the admired masters of the universe we originally knew ourselves to be. Indeed, many of our adolescent patients are in treatment precisely because of their habit of manipulating people as if others were extensions of the patient's wishes rather than separate human beings. Surely therapists should show less psychopathy and narcissism than their patients.

I think we must use manipulation with some patients—out-of-control adolescent patients among them—because we must work with patients where they are, not demand that they become capable of types of interaction they are manifestly not capable of before we agree to treat them. One way to describe the manner in which disturbed adolescents are disturbed is to note that they are repeatedly drawn to only one or two patterns of interaction through which they compulsively act out certain experiences of self and other (cf. Leary 1957). One possible measure of mental health is whether we have a broad pattern of self–other interactions available to us, and can therefore be flexible across changing situations and persons, versus whether we must repeatedly compress our experiences into a small handful of self–other patterns that do not really fit the external situation. It is one thing, for instance, to be cynical and angry with a corrupt and ruthless boss, but it is a different matter (a pathological matter) if we reflexively react with cynicism and anger to almost anyone with any authority. The out-of-control adolescent has lost access to the wide range of possibilities that define human experience and has instead become locked into a narrow band of options for experiencing self and other.

The therapist will also be experienced within this narrow band, and sooner rather than later the troubled adolescent will interact in a way that shows how distorted his or her experience of therapy is. At that point the therapist has a choice, to respond either directly or indirectly—that is, manipulatively. It is good practice to try a direct intervention, such as confrontation, first. Unhappily, it is not likely to succeed but will be lost in the distortions it was designed to address. If therapists hope to open up new possibilities for the patient, they will have to cut off the patient's access to the distorted self–other experience. Most of the time, cutting off access entails some manipulation.

Perhaps this seems too extreme a solution. After all, we are simply talking about resistance, and every patient, no matter the age, comes to therapy with resistances. The better part of a century ago, Nunberg (1926) wrote that the aims of the therapist are flatly opposed to the (unconscious and therefore genuine) aims of the patient, at least at the outset of treatment, and that the patient's true aims do not promote the treatment. Nunberg wrote about psychoanalytic patients, but his remark is certainly true of almost any patient in any type of verbal therapy. The psychodynamic schools of thought have long been aware of this and train us to look for and deal with resistance. We can do this because most patients are able to form a so-called alliance with treatment, agreeing in some fashion to suspend pathology, as it were, and cooperate with the aims of treatment, even though those aims run counter to their own genuine, if unspoken, intentions.

Can out-of-control adolescent patients do this? Eventually, yes. Can they do it without some sort of specially tailored interventions aimed at their resistances? Generally speaking, no. My impression is that most clinicians sense this even if they are not sure how they ought to defeat their adolescent patient's resistance. Anecdotal evidence leads me to believe that the strategy most often used is to try to buddy up to the patient in some way, to indicate to the patient that the therapist is not like the parents and may in fact be on the patient's side, as it were, against the parents. There are several reasons that this attempt at seduction is the wrong approach, and this strategy will be discussed in more detail below. For now it is enough to refer to Dickes's (1975) thoroughly correct remark that it is a mistake to try to seduce patients into treatment. My point here is that many if not most therapists do try to maneuver or manipulate the adolescent into a treatment alliance, although the manipulation that is most often used is not the correct one.

The therapist's goal should be to find some way to establish a relationship in which the truth can be spoken or, as Kierkegaard (1846/1992) might have said, to find a relationship that addresses the patient in his or her subjectivity. Thus, the target of therapeutic interventions must be whatever stance the patient has adopted that precludes such a relationship. I refer, of course, to the five types of resistance outlined in the previous chapter. The therapist must try to maneuver or manipulate adolescent patients out of their preferred form of resistance.

The chief objection to the idea that adolescent patients must be manipulated out of resistance is the one briefly touched on earlier, the concept of a treatment alliance. Clearly, if patients can be helped to work through resistance with proper technique, overt manipulation need not be used. We should therefore think through the concept of a therapeutic alliance to see if it can be applied to out-of-control adolescents. If it can, then we need not resort to the admittedly distasteful idea of manipulation.

THE CONCEPT OF AN ALLIANCE WITH THE PATIENT

The idea of an alliance between therapist and patient that carries them through difficult periods comes from psychoanalytic thought. As might be expected, Freud was the first to explore the subject. I think it is fair to say that he could not bring himself completely to decide whether the factors that lead to cooperation are rational or irrational, whether they are based, that is, on the patient's judgment and correct apprehension of reality or on the patient's unconscious fantasies, wishes, and fears.

Very early, Freud (Breuer and Freud 1895) remarked that "we make of the patient a collaborator" (p. 282) whose receptivity to insight overcomes resistance. This sounds rational, as if cooperation is built on the patient's ability to step back from the urge to resist change and instead consider the insights offered by analysis. In *An Outline of Psychoanalysis* Freud (1940) wrote of the motivation for treatment that comes from the patient's suffering (and the hope for relief) and also of the fact that treatment can awaken an intellectual curiosity. These, of course, are rational, or reality-based, factors.

However, Freud (1912a) also attributed the patient's cooperation to transference, that is, to the patient's displacement onto the therapist of certain experiences, expectations, fears, and fantasies built around other figures in the patient's life. In this case, transference may lead the patient to feel warmly attached to the therapist and to hold grossly unrealistic expectations of therapy. As Freud (1940) wrote, transference sweeps away "the patient's rational aim of becoming healthy and free from his ailments" (p. 172). The patient may cooperate with treatment out of hope of winning the therapist's approval and love or because the therapist is experienced as a beloved (or feared) parent. In any case, if cooperation is built on transference, it is irrational. Because it leads to cooperation, though, Freud (1912a) regarded this sort of positive transference as "unobjectionable" even if it is not realistic.

The question of whether the patient's cooperation is rational or irrational in nature is an important one. Do most patients—and here we are talking about adult patients—try to cooperate with therapy through the better angels of their natures or, rather, through the influence of the very conflicts, wishes, and fantasies that drove them to need therapy in the first place? If the latter is the case, then the alliance is built on the ways irrational aims can influence the patient's behavior, which is to say it is built on the patient's pathology. After all, if the patient cooperates with treatment because he or she unconsciously seeks the therapist's approval, the therapist is being asked to gratify infantile wishes.

If this is so, shouldn't it be a focus of treatment? Freud did not think so. He viewed the patient's attachment to the therapist as terribly useful, no matter that it was built on infantile needs. He argued, indeed, that the therapist ought not try to wrestle with the patient's pathology until a firm attachment existed (e.g., Freud 1912a), thereby declaring that an attachment built on infantile needs was a necessary precondition for treatment. In effect Freud advised therapists to be willing to employ some of the patient's pathological needs against other pathological needs, not going out of the way to point out to the patient that whatever alliance existed was the result of such irrational forces.

The analytically oriented therapist is, in effect, saying to the patient that infantile needs, wishes, and fantasies that stand in the way of treatment (resistances) must be faced and worked through. The therapist is not saying, however, that one of the forces that will make this possible is the existence in the therapeutic relationship of other infantile needs, wishes, and fantasies. Certainly one of the goals of treatment may be to work these through as well eventually, but this is not said at first—at least not by any therapist who wishes to keep his or her momentary advantage.

A certain amount of discomfort with the situation might be expected from writers trying to sort through this "paradox" (Friedman 1988). Thus, those who worked with or followed Freud tried to find a more rational footing for treatment. Greenson (1967) and also Dickes (1967, 1975), for example, distinguished the *working* alliance from the *treatment* alliance. The former was described as reality-based and rational. It was built on the real relationship between the therapist and patient, the patient's discomfort from symptoms, and the patient's ability to maintain an intellectual grasp of what treatment required.

The treatment alliance was a broader concept. It included the working alliance and also the irrational elements driving the relationship, such as those neurotic needs and infantile wishes that might cause the patient to feel connected to the therapist. The idea is that irrational elements gradually leave the relationship as the patient matures and grows healthier. As Dickes (1975) wrote, "Affection based on unreal evaluation of the [therapist] diminishes gradually, as a rule, during the course of treatment" (p. 21). In a successful case, the patient eventually cooperates with the therapist for rational, reality-level reasons.

Will the distinction between a reality-based alliance and a neurosis-based alliance hold up? Friedman (1988) implied that the motivation for making this distinction in the first place is that therapists are uncomfortable with the idea that they are trading on the patient's infantile wishes and needs. Why should this be a source of discomfort? Because it is dishonest, albeit benignly so, to accept some irrational motives without interpretation while attacking others. Thus, the treatment alliance is founded on a certain dishonesty on the therapist's part. It was after seeing or at least sensing this state of affairs that some writers went on to propose that there might be a reality-based alliance and that the irrationally based treatment alliance is not all there is. It would be a more comfortable situation if this were so.

If it is not so, then the treatment alliance actually sounds quite a bit like a manipulation of the patient. After all, the therapist is picking and choosing pretty carefully just how much to tell the patient and is making that judgment on the basis of what will help the case along. The ugly question to be asked, then, is not whether manipulation is involved in overcoming adolescent resistance but whether every overcoming of resistance in any patient does not involve manipulation. The only thing different about manipulation of out-of-control adolescents is that conventional therapeutic technique will not work. It is not so much that manipulation is needed but that a special manipulation is needed.

My argument, then, is that there is nothing terribly unusual about manipulating patients past early forms of resistance. The formation of any treatment alliance presupposes this. The only question to be addressed is whether special techniques are needed to form some sort of alliance with adolescent patients.

FORMING A TREATMENT ALLIANCE
WITH ADOLESCENT PATIENTS

The way one tries to form a workable alliance with the patient will depend on what one takes to be the source of resistance. The source of resistance in adolescent patients seems to have been thought through most thoroughly by psychoanalytically informed writers. A host of analysts (Aarons 1970, Deutsch 1944, Geleerd 1957, Katan 1935) have written that the major cause of initial resistance is that the adolescent patient will experience the therapist as the parents' replacement, an idea alluded to earlier. Adolescents rarely come for treatment on their own but come at the behest of the parents, and so it is an easy conclusion that the therapist stands in for the parents in some way. The patient will presumably be inclined therefore to resist the therapist out of the desire to establish some independence from the parents. In such a situation, the therapist would instantly be in the same relationship to the patient as are the parents, a kind of generalized, nonspecific transference.

To the great credit of analytic writers, they have *not* gone on to say that the solution is to help the patient see that the therapist is not like the parents, nor have they concluded that therapy would go smoother if there were no equation of therapist with parents. This would be the error mentioned earlier in this chapter, that therapists may try to seduce patients into treatment by taking their side against the parents or by otherwise emphasizing that the therapist is not a representative of the adult world. Therapists who make this mistake assume that the chief resistance to treatment is grounded in the patient's equation of the therapist with the parents and that if this equation were undone, the resistance would also be undone.

In fact, Harley (1970) has argued that the reverse may actually be true. She suggests that most adolescents, and early adolescents in particular, will be frightened of therapists who emphasize their nonparental role or offer themselves as a means of pushing away the parents. The argument goes that adolescents are, after all, fighting to contain themselves as much as they are pushing away the parents. They are trying not to get carried away with the surges of emotion and energy that this time of life regularly visits upon them. The parents are likely to be seen as resources against these disturbing inward whirlpools of impulse and affect; even though the adolescent may wish to show independence from these external rule-givers, they are nonetheless seen as bulwarks against the chaos within. If the therapist emphasizes being different from the parents, the patient may well see him or her as someone who is on the side of the inner disorganization. It is therefore countertherapeutic for therapists to emphasize that they are not parental figures. According to this line of thought, the patient will not be relieved and may in fact become even more suspicious.

Indeed, the adolescent's internal chaos forms another source of resistance. Harley (also Aarons 1970, Fraiberg 1955) argued that even the most rebellious adolescent wants to regain control over the inner storm. Adolescents are therefore not eager to explore their intense feelings and impulses. Even the process of putting these feelings into words may feel terribly threatening to the patient, and this perceived threat leads the adolescent to resist treatment. By inviting the patient to articulate and explore issues that are charged with conflict, therapy may run counter to the patient's almost desperate desire to suppress these issues.

Of course, there is also a healthy side to the patient's initial resistance. Blos (1983), for instance, has said that resistance implies that the patient's ego wants to protect an established and familiar life against the prospect of change. If the patient is to have any strength at all, he or she must be able to offer such resistance. Its absence, in fact, would be alarming. Similarly, Fraiberg (1955) believed that the patient's negativism is a healthy defense against the loss of self that would follow a too sudden surrender to another person. Thus, even an adolescent in pain can be counted on to resist help, loss of self being feared more than the pain.

The situation might look something like this to an analytically oriented therapist, then. On the one hand, the patient will resist the treatment simply because the therapist is associated with the parents. On the other hand, the adolescent does not want to lose control of the inner world, which has become more threatening with the upsurge of the sexual and aggressive energies associated with puberty. He or she therefore will not necessarily reach out to a therapist even if the therapist is not confused with the parents; the therapeutic process itself may prove threatening.

Given these considerations, it is easy to see why the question of a treatment alliance has been difficult. The aims of puberty, as Fraiberg (1955) has said, are at odds with the aims of therapy. If the adolescent ego is trying to resist the influence of the drives, therapy tries to loosen the defenses. If adolescence is a time of secrecy from adults, therapy pries into secrets. If the adolescent sometimes fears for his or her sanity, the therapist must seem to be continually questioning the patient's sanity. In other words, the sources of resistance appear rather normal or age-appropriate (Evans 1976). Anna Freud (1958) argued that the nature of the problem was indeed adolescence itself, that it is a time of life when there is too little ego strength for any deep therapy.

These arguments are hard to evaluate. They seem compelling, and yet I am not sure that they are helpful, at least not in discussing the out-of-control patient. The conclusion we are perilously close to reaching is that it would be sick, or at least age-inappropriate, for an adolescent patient to achieve a treatment alliance. This conclusion may well follow if we start with the ideas just summarized, that it is difficult to get an adolescent invested in treatment because of certain normal developmental issues. Yet how can we not start from that idea? There at least seems to be something uniquely difficult about adolescent patients that separates them from adult patients and also from child patients. Surely the source of the difficulty lies in the nature of adolescence as a developmental stage, and we are therefore right to look at developmental themes.

Perhaps the question of whether this is the right approach can be better answered if we look at the solutions offered in the literature for achieving a treatment alliance. Fraiberg (1955) suggested that many problems will disappear if a positive transference can be elicited, although she acknowledged the difficulty of that task. Harley (1970) counseled a steady focus on the patient's inner world with the idea that the therapist can help the patient control his or her feelings so that they do not control the patient. Aarons (1970) argued that neutrality was essential and that the therapist must be nonparental. In fact, Aarons suggested that therapists should respond to the patient's attempt to parentify the therapist by showing that it is a disruption of treatment. Evans (1976) was not sure anything special was needed: "I should have to conclude that the only technique required for 'fostering' the therapeutic alliance is that of effective analysis" (p. 222).

These do not seem to be radical proposals, and in fact they sound a lot like "business as usual." After outlining the ways that adolescent developmental tasks complicate achieving a working alliance, these authors then propose nothing really special for establishing that alliance. This is hard to accept. If the usual therapeutic techniques were enough to help the adolescent become invested in treatment, it seems unlikely the question would have come up in the first place.

It may simply be the case that adolescents who can survive in analysis are better integrated than the out-of-control patients who are the subject of this book. In any event, it is not my impression that age-appropriate developmental tasks are the primary obstacles in establishing a working relationship with such patients. Indeed, my impression is that these patients are rather far from age-appropriate tasks and are trying (if anything) to avoid them. Whereas it is normal for an adolescent to push away the parents as burgeoning sexuality makes the parents into incestuous objects, out-of-control adolescents are often trying to preserve an infantile object tie.

This issue bears discussing in more detail. As just reviewed, two sources of adolescent resistance have been proposed in the psychoanalytic literature. The first is that the patient is trying to get away from the parents, and the therapist will be equated with the parents. This line of thought comes from two related arguments in psychoanalytic thought. One argument is that adolescence revives the oedipal struggle or, if it is too much to say that it is revived, that oedipal issues must be revisited in light of the teenager's burgeoning sexuality (Aarons 1971, Eissler 1958, Geleerd 1957, Jacobson 1961). They must be revisited because the solutions that worked during the oedipal period are rendered inoperable by puberty.

The oedipal age child had to repress sexual and hostile impulses toward the parents in order to preserve age-appropriate attachments and dependency; the child surrendered sexual and aggressive ambitions toward the parents that were simply unrealistic in light of the child's physical inferiority. In place of these unrealistic aims, the child gained a comfortable dependency on the parents that was in fact needed for proper growth. However, the adolescent's physical maturation makes sexual and aggressive wishes increasingly more realistic. The old oedipal bargain that was, as it were, struck with the parents ("I will not play an adult role with you, and in return I get to depend on you") thereby becomes moot. The adolescent can no longer depend on the parents as during childhood; more distance is needed. Continued dependency would, according to this line of thought, excite the adolescent to incestuous wishes. To fend off incest, the adolescent must push the parents away.

The second psychoanalytic argument that seeks to explain why adolescents push away their parents (and many parental surrogates) is similar to the first. It is that adolescence is a time of struggle between progressive and regressive desires, between desires to become mature and independent on the one hand and desires to return to infantile dependency on the other (Deutsch 1944; A. Freud 1958; Jacobson 1961, Lampl-de Groot 1960). The adolescent is trying to get free of relationships that were crucial to growing up but serve only to compromise the eventual goal of leaving home. The parents must be rejected because the adolescent is highly ambivalent about renouncing childhood dependency with its satisfactions and pleasures. Precisely because the adolescent is much tempted to move backwards instead of forward, the parents are vigorously rejected until the youth feels more confident of the ability to break away and resist regressive urges.

The two arguments are substantially the same. The first is made from the standpoint of the oedipal struggle, while the second is made from the perspective of ego psychology, but both emphasize that the battle is between the desires for infantile satisfactions and for maturity. The parents are rejected in both models because they tempt the adolescent to go backwards. Presumably the therapist, standing in for the parents, is resisted for the same reason. If the primary reason for resistance in therapy is that it is age-appropriate to resist parental influence, then therapy is resisted because the adolescent patient wants to move forward and cannot trust the pleasures of becoming dependent on the therapist.

The problem with this position is that it is the reverse of what we find with out-of-control adolescents. These are not youths who are trying to move forward toward independence but who are committed to maintaining what in psychoanalytic thought would be called infantile object relations. Even those who are most rebellious and seemingly resistant to their parents are in fact fighting off only that aspect of the parents that represents adult cause-and-effect reality. At the same time they are seeking to preserve a world in which the mother of physical contact is always available to praise, satisfy, and protect them.

Consequently a therapeutic technique built on the notion that the chief resistance to be found in adolescent treatment is somewhat age-appropriate is bound to be wrong. The idea that business as usual or, as Evans (1976) said, "effective analysis" is enough seems to me to be off the mark if we are talking about patients who are not wrestling with age-appropriate tasks but who are trying hard to *avoid* age-appropriate tasks. By and large, out-of-control adolescents, employing the patterns of resistance outlined in the previous chapter, are not ambivalent about their direction. This is why they can be so committed to their resistance and why in turn the therapist can and must respond single-mindedly to the resistance at first: these patients have already made their decision, and it is to move backward or at least to cling to regressive ways of experiencing the world.

We will arrive at the same conclusion if we examine the second proposed source of adolescent resistance described in the psychoanalytic literature. The first source was that the parents become more dangerous as oedipal issues are revived by puberty. The second source is that adolescents feel pressed by internal chaos and fight to preserve their emotional equilibrium by avoiding highly charged issues. Consequently, a therapy session can look like an invitation to give in to the emotional tidal wave the patient is already just barely keeping in check.

This viewpoint is not essentially different from the ego psychology argument just given. We have just reviewed an argument from ego psychology to the effect that the teenager is trapped between regressive and progressive wishes and is trying to ally with the latter. The idea that adolescents are fighting off internal chaos is at heart an argument that ego and instinct are again at war, that the fragile truce between these two parts of the personality reached in latency has broken down (A. Freud 1958), and the adolescent seeks to take ego's side.

The reply I would give to this argument is essentially what I argued earlier, that out-of-control adolescents do not appear to me to be trying to *master* the surge of instinct but, rather, to *satisfy* it and *preserve* it. As I will describe in the next chapter, these patients seek to maintain the fantasy that they can remain the admired and powerful infants of fusion and that they do not have to surrender infantile satisfactions in the interest of growing up.

Consequently, we are back at square one in an attempt to trace what is necessary for forming some sort of working relationship with resistant adolescents. My position is that we must be prepared to manipulate the out-of-control adolescent out of the period of initial resistance. Further, it is not only out-of-control adolescents who require some manipulation on the part of the therapist. Indeed, the usual technique used in the dynamic therapies to establish a working relationship rests on a benign manipulation. However, that technique will not lead to an alliance with out-of-control youths. Consequently, some more focused manipulation is needed.

PRINCIPLES OF MANIPULATION WITH OUT-OF-CONTROL ADOLESCENTS

Sprince (1971) gives an excellent example of the basic principles of benign manipulation when she outlines her work with an early adolescent boy. This patient felt that his mother's health required him to be sick; he was not therefore able to endorse treatment, since that would have required him to endorse health and maturity. Such an endorsement would have created a loyalty conflict between what was in his best interests and what was in his mother's (as he saw it). Sprince saw that he could not enter into a treatment alliance even to the point of agreeing to come to sessions. She therefore authoritatively told him that treatment was necessary and that he must comply.

This approach made the treatment possible. The boy was committed to passivity, and the therapist took advantage of this. Thus, the tactic that made treatment possible relied on the pathological passivity that treatment sought to cure. However paradoxical this may sound, it is not as paradoxical as insisting that the boy endorse the process that would lead him to (as he saw it) betray and harm his mother at a time when his life turned on preventing such a thing. Such an insistence would essentially demand that the patient be on the road to getting well before he was allowed into therapy. Sprince manipulated the patient, I think, and this was the only way this patient was able to engage in a helpful treatment.

Manipulating the adolescent patient first depends on being able to step back from the interaction in order to gain some cognitive understanding of the patient's resistance. The patient is, after all, trying to involve the therapist in his or her resistance, that is, in his or her preferred pattern of dealing with others. In the case Sprince described, the patient was trying to avoid any genuine interaction altogether, hiding behind his passivity. If the therapist gets caught up in the patient's preferred method of dealing with (or avoiding dealing with) others, nothing can be gained. Therefore the therapist must first of all step back and begin to tease out the ways the patient is trying to defeat the therapeutic process.

From the understanding gained by stepping back, the therapist must then try to determine what sort of interaction would be incompatible with the patient's resistance. In the case Sprince (1971) presented, the boy's resistance was built on his having jettisoned autonomy, on his having surrendered the ability to choose his course for himself. At first glance it might seem that his loyalty to his mother—the way he had committed himself to saving his mother (as he saw the matter) over all else—was the key to the case. While this set of issues was undeniably at the heart of the case, it was not the key to overcoming resistance. Rather, the key to the boy's resistance was: What interpersonal stance followed from his decision to sacrifice his life for his mother's? The answer, of course, was *passivity*. Sprince realized this, and realized too that she could take advantage of the patient's passivity in order to bring him to sessions. She simply ordered him, in effect, to attend sessions. Although he did not wish to do this and preferred to hide behind his passivity, Sprince's authoritative stance put him in an impossible bind: either he could remain passive (as he must if he were to be committed to his mother) and attend sessions, or he could defy Sprince (but in the process break out of his passivity into willfulness). He could not both remain passive and at the same time avoid sessions.

As Sprince's case illustrates, once therapists have found an interaction incompatible with a patient's chosen form of resistance, they must assume a posture that makes that interaction possible. In this case Sprince became autocratic and controlling, traits undoubtedly at odds with the values she would otherwise endorse as an analyst. Similarly, other therapists may find themselves playing roles, as it were, given to them by the moment—given to them, that is, by the type of interaction they must have with the patient if they are to overcome the initial resistance. If Sprince had not been willing to be authoritative with her patient, she could not have created an inter-action that led to his presence at sessions. In the same way, thera-pists must slip into and out of roles that create an interaction incom-patible with the patient's resistance.

BRIEF CLINICAL EXAMPLE

A 15-year-old girl had been angry with her mother for several years and had behaved in ways that bothered her mother quite a bit. She refused to attend school for almost an entire year, dated a much older man who occasionally beat her, and used drugs. These be-haviors actually cost the patient much more than they cost her mother, but the fact that they worried her mother was enough to let her persist. The mother had a demanding job and had to travel often, and she found that she simply could not control the girl with her limited time and energy. Outpatient therapy was tried repeat-edly with no result; eventually the girl would simply refuse to go. Finally at her wit's end, the mother told the girl to try therapy in earnest or else be sent to a long-term residential program.

The patient arrived for her first session and said in a matter-of-fact manner that she was there only because of her mother's threat and had no intention of doing anything other than wasting her mother's money. She outlined some of her guerrilla warfare against her mother after the therapist asked what had led the mother to make such an ultimatum. She ended her fairly brief summary by saying that she hated her mother, hated her father (divorced from the mother and living in another state) even more, and wanted only to be old enough to move out and make it on her own.

The therapist asked about the wisdom of her approach, pointing out the obvious, that the patient had little to show for her long battle with the mother, who seemed still to be able to control the patient when the chips were down. The patient replied that she did not care, regretted nothing, and planned to continue her tactics. She reiterated that she wanted nothing to do with therapy and planned to waste sessions. Her attitude was challenging and belligerent, and the therapist felt the temptation to enter a power struggle or to show the girl who was the boss by furthering admission to residential care. There was a "you can't make me do anything" quality to the patient that the therapist could not quite tune out.

The therapist reasoned that the patient would be compelled to resist whatever he proposed. The patient had already defined him as the mother's extension, and she was determined to give her mother no satisfaction at all. He therefore switched sides and began to endorse the patient's strategy, saying it made a lot of sense under the circumstances and must have been very satisfying. He added that he might even be able to suggest ways to continue the battle that the girl had not yet thought of.

The patient immediately objected that he could not be serious and without waiting for reassurance on the question began to outline all that her strategy had cost her. She noted she had made no friends during the year, was far behind in school, was in trouble with the courts, and had been used by her boyfriend. The therapist replied that all this might be true but that some cost must be expected if she was to show her mother who was the boss. He added that she also had the great satisfaction of hurting her mother and making her life, as the patient described it, "a living hell."

The patient then began to cry, saying it had hurt her to see her mother cry. She said that in fact she loved her mother and wished they could have some sort of reconciliation. She then described again all that the last several years had cost her and said that her behavior had been "utterly stupid." She said that she wanted to change but did not know how.

The therapist briefly considered agreeing with the patient and offering to help her change. He thought, however, that the patient was still essentially in an oppositional stance and that everything sensible the patient had said was simply a reflexive act of defiance against his earlier paradoxical suggestions. He therefore said that he was confused and did not know what to say, that he thought he had understood the girl and made sensible recommendations that he was still prepared to back up. As the session ended, he added that the patient seemed so oppositional that he doubted any good could come of sessions since she would obviously reject his best ideas out of hand.

This session gave the therapist several useful pieces of information. The session confirmed that the patient saw the therapist as the mother's extension, was engaged in a paranoid-like resistance, and would react in a defiant fashion to almost any intervention. The session also revealed that the patient had a rather different side to her, one capable of better judgment and tender feelings, but that this side too was likely to be expressed only in the context of defiance.

Beyond this information, the session also showed a possible way out of the patient's resistance. The therapist discovered that adopting a paradoxical approach (e.g., Fisch et al. 1982, Goldberg 1973, Haley 1986) could force the patient's resistance to serve the cause of clearer thinking. This patient had already demonstrated the ability to wait a long time and to behave in a self-defeating (if not self-destructive) way in order to get back at her mother. There is no reason to believe she would not have done the same thing in therapy, especially given her history of multiple failed treatments. Consequently, an approach aimed at her resistances seemed very much in order. The paradoxical approach that was chosen bypassed, or altered the nature of, the patient's oppositionality. Instead of fighting off the therapist as a representative of adult reality, the patient became an advocate of that reality. Through resisting the therapist, the patient became a little healthier. Without the therapist's paradoxical stance, the patient would undoubtedly have resisted the therapist through becoming a little sicker instead.

It may be objected (correctly) that the events of a single session mean little. Getting a patient to say several healthy things really changes nothing with an out-of-control patient, and therefore one might argue that the approach used to produce these results may not be better than a conventional approach. The problem with this objection is that it holds for all therapeutic approaches to resistance, including conventional approaches. If the therapist had used conventional technique and elicited several adaptive, ego-building remarks from the patient, the results would be no more meaningful. The question to be answered is not what approach will produce quick results in these types of cases—no approach will do that. Rather, the question is what approaches might offer therapists ways to attack adolescent resistance. In the above example, the patient's resistance was modified; it was made to produce more mature thinking. Whenever a patient can be brought to more adaptive thinking, resistance is being undermined.

CHAPTER 3

THEORETICAL FOUNDATIONS: THE NARCISSISTIC CORE

THE NARCISSISTIC CORE AND THE RESISTANCE STAGE OF TREATMENT

We must distinguish the type of resistance shown by out-of-control adolescents from the underlying pathology. Resistance may take any of the five forms outlined in Chapter 1, but the underlying pathology is, I believe, more unitary. The underlying pathology will probably be hidden in the early stages of treatment, when resistance dominates the clinical picture. If the case goes well, though, the therapist should eventually see elements of pathological narcissism underneath the initial resistance. In my experience, most out-of-control adolescents suffer some variant of narcissistic pathology.

Clinicians should not confuse narcissistic *resistance* with narcissistic *pathology*. My thesis is that almost all out-of-control adolescents suffer from narcissistic pathology—not only those who show narcissistic resistance. Thus, even those patients who show other forms of resistance will eventually show narcissistic issues after the initial resistance has been addressed. In addition, therapists should note that proper handling of narcissistic resistance does nothing to address the underlying narcissistic pathology: if a patient shows narcissistic resistance and this is handled successfully, the patient will still have underlying narcissistic issues waiting to be addressed in the later stages of treatment.

This raises the question whether it is important to be aware of the patient's underlying issues in the early phase of treatment. If the initial resistance has little to do with core pathology, do clinicians need to be aware of core pathology during the resistance phase? In my opinion it is necessary. The first reason for this is largely practical and has to do with the clinician's morale or, rather, with the clinician's efforts to keep from becoming demoralized.

Out-of-control adolescents are difficult to treat without feeling that the therapy is futile. The initial resistance can be so dogged and hard to resolve that therapists may well find themselves feeling hopeless. Such a feeling may reflect projective identification, as the patient induces in the therapist some aspect of the patient's self-experience that cannot be integrated. In this case the patient's sense of being helpless in the face of problems is "given" to the therapist, with the implied question of whether the therapist can handle the feeling better than the patient was able to handle it. The feeling can be overwhelming for the therapist. Even on a reality level these patients are hard to deal with and tax a therapist's energy and ingenuity. When the effect of projective identification is added to realistic reasons to feel discouraged, the therapist may give up on the case too soon, or may put forth only a half-hearted effort, feeling the case is already lost anyway.

Anything that might help therapists keep their wits about them in the face of discouragement is therefore helpful. In this case, therapists should try to sort through their subjective sense of futility, trying to separate what is realistic from what is their own reaction to the patient's projected self-image. Therapists must be aware that out-of-control patients are trying to preserve a grandiose view of themselves in which they are their own ego ideal and are therefore motivated to jettison anything that might undermine grandiosity. It is a threat to grandiosity to feel helpless in the face of problems, and the therapist is, in effect, asked to experience helplessness on the patient's behalf.

Beyond the practical matter of the therapist's morale, the therapist's reaction also plays a role in the patient's pathology. If therapists allow themselves to be defeated by the projected self-image, the patient's pathology is reinforced. Not only is grandiosity left unchallenged, but the patient's fear of the completely human experience of weakness is also strengthened. Therapists therefore must try to understand their own feelings of futility in light of the patient's underlying narcissistic pathology. Such an effort may help therapists contain and modify the patient's projected, unwanted self-image (Ogden 1982), thereby representing for the patient the possibility of a more human, integrated self.

A further reason therapists should be aware of the patient's underlying narcissistic pathology is that there will be opportunities to lay a foundation for later work on narcissistic issues. Even during the resistance phase of treatment, the therapist will have opportunities to learn how the patient and the parents interact. This information will be valuable later, even though there is little to be done with it while resistance is strong. The therapist should keep the dynamics of pathological narcissism in mind while hearing about the patterns of family interaction. This allows for useful hypotheses about how the parents' behavior with the patient may have contributed to underlying pathology and therefore useful hypotheses about later interventions.

Consequently, therapists working with out-of-control youths should be aware of the underlying pathology, even while the patient is still in the resistance phase of treatment and therefore unlikely to show that pathology directly. There is little point in trying to speak to the underlying pathology during the resistance phase; the out-of-control patient is not likely to tolerate an honest exchange on those issues as long as his or her preferred mode of resistance is available. Thus it is a mistake to try to address the patient's underlying narcissistic issues even if those become visible early in a treatment. Therapists must be content to realize that these issues will probably be available later, that they will prove to be core issues with most out-of-control adolescents.

NARCISSISM, THE OEDIPAL STAGE,
AND THE EGO IDEAL

The narcissism of the out-of-control adolescent has been noted both in clinical literature (e.g., Aichhorn 1964, Marohn 1977, Sherwood 1990) and, probably more frequently, in clinical encounters. Even the most demoralized and depressed among these patients refuse to let the therapist make any impact—generally not out of conflict, fear, or anxiety but out of a grandiose conviction that the patient has nothing to learn from therapy or from adults in general. This grandiosity is typically accompanied by other narcissistic traits, including a narrowly egocentric cognitive focus, inability to empathize, a tendency to see others as an extension of the self, excessive entitlement, and pride that is built on infantile omnipotence rather than on realistic accomplishments. The patient's omnipotence and grandiosity are protected by a capacity to deny the significance of most long-term consequences and usually by an illusion of self-sufficiency.

As noted, these traits have been discussed in the literature. However, such discussions have typically focused on delinquent youths, who tend to be more obviously narcissistic than other out-of-control patients. It is therefore important to realize that the narcissistic qualities just described hold for almost all out-of-control adolescents. Some patients are too self-effacing or masochistic to be consciously grandiose or self-sufficient. These tend to attribute grandeur to an idealized other, perhaps a boyfriend or girlfriend or a gang or cult, through whom and in whose company they too enjoy this trait. Whether the patient is antisocial, self-endangering, affectively labile, schizoid, or paranoid, there is usually a narcissistic core to the pathology of the out-of-control adolescent. In some patients the form of resistance is congenial to the underlying pathology, and it is fairly easy to see narcissistic traits early in treatment. My point is that even when these traits are hidden, they are in most cases still present.

Pathological narcissism has received much attention over the past thirty years. The ideas of such writers as Kernberg (1975), Kohut (1971), Masterson (1981), and Rinsley (1982) are by now well known to every serious student in the field. While most of the work on pathological narcissism has centered on adult patients, there have been efforts to study adolescent populations. Rinsley (1980) and Masterson (1972, 1980) have made specific studies of adolescent patients, including some adolescents who could be described as out-of-control youths. Additionally, some writers have tried to apply Kohut's ideas specifically to the problems of delinquent and aggressive youth (e.g., Marohn 1977, Willock 1986, 1987). To this point, however, there is no consensus in the field on how to conceptualize the narcissism of the out-of-control adolescent and therefore no consensual basis for devising therapeutic strategies.

Advances during the 1970s and 1980s in our understanding of narcissism were primarily the result of examining the preoedipal determinants of that condition. This focus corresponded to a general shift in psychoanalytic thought away from the oedipal struggle and toward the psychology of the first few years of life. Those authors already mentioned who studied adolescent patients likewise focused on preoedipal themes. By contrast, this chapter proposes a return to certain aspects of the oedipal struggle as the best framework for understanding the out-of-control adolescent's narcissistic pathology. More specifically, the adolescent patient's narcissism may be seen as a type of ego ideal pathology, the result of the child's failure to project infantile omnipotence onto the parents (Freud 1912b), thereby inhibiting development of the ego ideal (Freud 1914).

As with other aspects of narcissism in out-of-control adolescents, most of the attention paid to the ego ideal has come from those who have sought to understand delinquents. Aichhorn (1964), for example, argued that delinquent youth lack an ego ideal. He found that poor identifications with the parents lead to the absence of this part of the personality; in turn, this absence makes socialization virtually impossible, and antisocial behavior follows. More recently, Rinsley (1982) made a similar argument while discussing patients he regarded as borderline adolescents showing behavioral problems. He observed that many contemporary parents lack ideals and values of their own and that such parents cannot serve as ideals for their children. Consequently, they cannot challenge their children's natural narcissism, for they have nothing on which to ground their authority over their children's wishes and impulses.

These conclusions do not go to the heart of the matter, however. As long as the ego ideal is studied only in the context of behaviorally disordered youth, its role in controlling behavior will, of course, be figural. Behavior control, however, is not the ego ideal's most important function. There is a much broader role, one that applies to all out-of-control adolescents, even those whose behavior is not especially delinquent.

The most important function of the ego ideal is its role in motivating the child to grow up. The ego ideal is the tool by which the child embraces the idea of his or her own psychological development. Chasseguet-Smirgel (1985) suggests that the ego ideal serves as a "hope" or "promise" that motivates the child to exchange the immediate gratifications of infantile dependence for the sublimated and delayed gratifications of successive developmental stages. In brief, children are asked to give up infantile megalomania, or our natural grandiosity and self-centeredness, and recognize the parents' superiority—not only their physical superiority but also the primacy of the adult construction of the world. As children we may envy this superiority and primacy, but we take the sting out of the envy by seeing our own lost grandiosity in the parents. By surrendering infantile omnipotence to the parents, we make them into our ego ideal. By growing up to become like them, we hope to attain for ourselves their power and prerogatives.

It is perhaps one of the miracles of civilization that vast numbers of people can be induced to abandon the pleasures of infantile omnipotence in favor of the frustrations of growing up. The ego ideal plays the critical role in this process by promising the child that he or she can eventually become like the object whose power and prerogatives the child now envies and takes as a model. The parents encourage the child to "project his ego ideal on to successively more evolved models," which pressures the child to "give up certain satisfactions . . . in order to acquire new ones" (Chasseguet-Smirgel 1985, p. 30).

It is no small thing the child is asked to surrender in exchange for the hope of becoming like the envied parent. Prior to birth we live in a world of coenesthesis with the mother (Grunberger 1989). It is a world of narcissistic perfection, without desire, where need is met even before it is experienced, and therefore a world without time or other boundary. While birth ends coenesthesis, the child is not ready to give up narcissistic perfection. As Grunberger argues, the child makes the transition from one primal fantasy to another: perfection is now attributed to the mother, who has the task of producing an approximation of the original milieu. At the breast the child is alone and merged with his or her universe, and instants of narcissistic perfection endure. The infant enjoys moments of omnipotence in which instinctual tensions are magically relieved and oneness with the mother is restored.

The growing child is called on to surrender this omnipotence, magic, and oneness in favor of history, that is, in favor of being thrown into evolving stages of development. Part of what calls on the child to do this comes from within, to be sure. It is the child's own idea, if I may put it that way, to crawl and then to walk and to become incrementally more autonomous. Yet we know how difficult it is for the child when it finally dawns that autonomy and merger with the mother travel different roads. Mahler's (Mahler et al. 1975) work on the rapprochement subphase of development chronicles the child's anguish at learning that the self is independent of the mother. The child is at pains to continue development, which takes the child toward reality and time. But the child also intends to preserve perfection or to cling to a world of wish and illusion. The "terrible twos" are simply the first of many signs that no one grows up happily.

It could be argued that we never completely surrender the hope of a return to our narcissistic perfection. It was Ferenczi's (1936) idea, and one at least partly endorsed by Freud (1926), that we continue to be driven by strong and persistent derivatives of our wish to return to mother–infant fusion. This idea changes how we must understand the Oedipus complex. Ferenczi treated Oedipus as a representative of the reality principle: his mother tried to divert him from the search for truth and made him promise, in effect, to be satisfied with make-believe. Jocasta therefore stands for illusion and the denial of adult reality (Grunberger 1989). Psychologically, this is the world of the mother: regression, wish fulfillment, magic, and oneness. By contrast, as Freud observed, the oedipal struggle begins for the son with the discovery that the father stands opposed to his wishes. The world of the father is the adult construction of reality, the world of cause and effect, time, separateness, and therefore guilt.

From this point of view the oedipal child's wish to usurp the place of the same-sex parent is not a desire to assume an adult's place but, rather, a derivative of a regressive impulse: the oedipal boy's desire for his mother and the oedipal girl's desire for a baby (with whom she can identify) by the father both echo a yearning for the perfection of mother–infant oneness. More than anything else, oedipal impulses represent a wish for the time when the child was his or her own ideal, basking in the admiring gaze of the mother of fusion (Chasseguet-Smirgel 1985).

The child's pursuit of such a wish rests on the maintenance of two denials that are typical of the oedipal period, namely, denial of the difference between the sexes and denial of the difference between adults and children (Chasseguet-Smirgel 1984). Each denial implies the other, and together they allow the illusion that the child is anatomically able to realize his or her oedipal wishes. If there are no differences between the generations, then there is nothing the rival parent can do which the child could not also do. The boy can hope to satisfy or complete his mother's life as well as the father could, and the girl can hope that she, like her mother, will receive a baby from the father. If there are no differences between the sexes, a child will do as well as an adult for a mate, and there is no cause to envy the rival parent or to acknowledge the rival's superiority.

These denials, and therefore the child's infantile grandiosity, are normally undone by the humiliating discovery of the child's physical inadequacy compared to the rival parent (Freud 1920). This humiliation begins with the recognition of differences between the sexes. It is well known that the sight of female genitalia can be upsetting to the oedipal boy. Freud (1924) regarded this as evidence of castration anxiety. However, something more traumatic than fear of castration may be involved. As McDougall (1972) points out, the sight of female genitalia may be upsetting chiefly because it deals a hard blow to the oedipal boy's narcissism: the mother's lack of a penis does not so much confirm the possibility of castration as it forces the child to recognize the role of the father's penis and the child's anatomical inability to fill that role (Chasseguet-Smirgel 1985, Grunberger 1989).

In classical psychoanalytic theory, the son gives up his oedipal strivings out of fear of the father (castration anxiety). This is not a satisfactory explanation, however. If the sole obstacle to incest is the father's ability to castrate his son, then the child's narcissism has not really been challenged. The child can restore the illusion of completeness if the reason for the oedipal failure is purely external. The child's immaturity is replaced with a prohibition from the outside. The boy could then keep the illusion that he actually could have satisfied his mother, thereby reuniting with his primary love object. In such a case the boy need not surrender his regressive wishes in favor of growing up.

The real problem for infantile grandiosity, then, is not prohibition by the parent of the opposite sex but recognition of the differences between adult and child bodies. The recognition of the difference between adults and children, and consequently between the sexes, decisively undermines the child's narcissism. The child had wanted to preserve the illusion of infantile omnipotence by returning to the perfection of mother–infant fusion. During the oedipal struggle the child's path to satisfying this wish is blocked by the rival parent's anatomical superiority. The oedipal child comes to envy the rival parent and then to project his or her own omnipotence onto the parent, thereby establishing the ego ideal (Freud 1912b, 1914).

With the formation of the ego ideal the child is turned away from regression and committed to history, that is, to development across time. The ego ideal propels the child to grow up, promising the boy that he can realize his regressive wish after a fashion by substituting genital intimacy for pregenital fusion. Similarly, the girl may hope to have a baby of her own when she grows up and enjoy vicariously her infant's symbiosis with her. The ego ideal thereby serves to inhibit regression and to promote psychological maturation.

Most out-of-control adolescents, however, have not moved beyond the regressive aspect of the oedipal struggle and continue to pursue the illusion of mother–infant fusion's omnipotent perfection. In general, such adolescents never underwent the (ultimately benevolent) humiliation of discovering their physical inadequacy compared to the rival parent during the oedipal period or did not undergo this humiliation in a benevolent manner. They had, therefore, no reason to envy an adult nor to submit to adult reality by projecting their own omnipotence onto the parents. A mature ego ideal is an impossibility in this case; the child remains his or her own ideal.

PATHOLOGY RELATED TO THE
FAILURE OF THE EGO IDEAL

The earliest memory of a 16-year-old boy, hospitalized for using and selling drugs and for other antisocial behaviors, illustrates the illusion of continued mother–infant perfection: "I swear I couldn't have been but a year old, maybe less. Most people don't think I can go back that far, but I can. I was lying in my mother's lap, and I remember we were at the top of the apartment building on the roof. And the sun was real bright, shining down on us, and she was holding me, and looking at me, and smiling, and it was so warm and bright. I just remember so clear her smiling down at me and the warm sun."

This patient's use of drugs allowed him to recreate the regressive state of mind contained in this fantasized memory. His identity was organized around the narcissistic image of glorious oneness with an admiring mother ("most people don't think I can go back that far, but I can"). His parents had divorced when he was barely more than an infant, and it appeared that his mother had turned to him as her reason for living. Consequently, he had no reason to project his omnipotence onto an adult and thus form an ego ideal. He felt he was already capable of completing and satisfying his mother's life without having to grow up. There was nothing for which he needed to envy an adult.

The failure to envy an adult implies the failure to surrender one of the two denials typical of the oedipal child. The out-of-control adolescent typically acknowledges the difference between the sexes but *continues to deny the difference between adults and children*. This absence of appropriate generational boundaries is one of the hallmarks of the out-of-control adolescent and is usually accompanied by an attitude of either disgust or angry despair toward the principal adults in the adolescent's life. While the oedipal denial of generational differences relies on the attendant denial of differences between the sexes, the out-of-control patient's denial of generational differences appears to rest on a too-early disillusionment with what might be termed the moral authority of adults.

Such disillusionment often, although not always, comes from one of four sources: parental reluctance to "win" the oedipal struggle; constitutional factors inhibiting internalization of parental standards; excessive parental sadism; or sexual abuse by an adult. Each of these general problems makes it difficult, if not impossible, for the growing child to surrender the oedipal denial of generational differences. The child then bursts into adolescence feeling entitled to the rights and privileges of adulthood without any corresponding willingness to sublimate sexual and aggressive impulses into socially appropriate channels, leading to poorly controlled behavior and, usually, substance abuse. Each of these four general sources of disillusionment with adults will be discussed in turn.

Parental Reluctance to Win the Oedipal Struggle

In many cases the parents of out-of-control youth seem to have been unwilling or even afraid to win the oedipal struggle. They simply failed to engage the child's narcissism during that critical period; consequently, appropriate generational boundaries were not established. Either of two scenarios seem to underlie such reluctance: first, the mother may turn to the child as the center of her emotional life, as with the child whose earliest memory is reported above; or, second, the parents may not be able to bring themselves to frustrate the child for fear of the child's anger with them. In either case the child's infantile megalomania is allowed to continue unchecked.

The first scenario appears to occur more regularly with parents suffering fairly extensive pathology themselves. Generally the father is not really present in the family life, leaving the mother emotionally if not physically alone. When the mother cannot tolerate such aloneness, she may turn to the child as a source of comfort and companionship, virtually elevating the child to the status of surrogate spouse. This effectively bypasses the oedipal struggle or undoes it, and the child's oedipal denial of generational differences goes unchallenged. In this situation, the child's behavior often becomes disordered shortly after the mother finds a new mate, enters therapy and starts to make personal changes, or for other reasons begins to treat the child more like a minor than a peer. The patient needs the mother to remain unstable or marginal in order to sustain the denial of generational differences. Any move toward maturity on the mother's part (e.g., abstinence by a formerly alcoholic mother) will seem to the child as either a narcissistic injury or an abandonment.

The second scenario typically occurs with parents who do not seem to suffer extensive psychopathology themselves but whose child-rearing skills are severely undermined by indecisiveness and self-doubt. In a sense we might say that these parents were victims of cultural anomie and moral uncertainty (Chessick 1977, Rinsley 1982); they found themselves full of doubts about how to discipline the child and took it as a bad sign when the child was angry with them. They were unable to bear the child's rage, feeling scared of what they had done and fearing that the child would not love them if they continued to evoke such frustration. In essence, they never saw the whole child, the child who is able to love and also to hate. Rather, they feared that the child's hatred toward them when they imposed limits would sweep away any love for them. In treatment it usually becomes clear that these parents were afraid of their own sadism as well as their child's. They projectively identified with the child's rage toward them and, over time, avoided engaging and challenging the child's narcissism because those encounters brought them too close to their own aggressiveness. Their child did not have to submit to adult (the parents') authority; the parents were too afraid of their authority to force submission.

Either situation is enough to derail formation of the ego ideal; children can neither admire nor trust parents who fail to check their omnipotence. As Rinsley (1982) noted, if the "child cannot repose his infantile megalomania in [his] parent, he cannot trust the parent" (p. 203). These children come to experience themselves as the emotional center of the household; they feel (often correctly) that they are running things. Even though they are quite capable of sudden outbursts of out-of-control behavior—generally when limits are suddenly imposed—they can also present themselves with unexpected poise, sometimes resembling miniature adults. Usually it is quite clear to anyone working with such children that they do not see a significant difference between the adults in their lives and themselves.

This apparently precocious maturity follows the child into adolescence. Youth whose parents failed to challenge their infantile omnipotence very often impress us initially with their seeming maturity, even though they may only be 14 or 15 years old. These patients can show a friendly poise and an attitude of effortless self-containment (see Modell 1984) that contrasts sharply with their histories of chaotic and impulsive behavior. This apparent maturity eventually can be recognized as illusory, however; when thwarted or frustrated, these youth typically lose all semblance of poise and affiliativeness. It then becomes clear that their seeming maturity stems from a precocious self-sufficiency, generally necessitated by their having sensed very early that, as one 16-year-old-girl put it, "My folks didn't know what they were doing," and so, "if anyone was going to be in charge it would have to be me."

Such patients are often willing to cooperate with a therapist as long as they can behave as if they were the therapist's peer—a behavior pattern that reflects the denial of generational differences. There is a price to be paid for accepting this pseudomaturity in therapy. Even though these patients generally become outraged when their pretense of adult status is challenged, they nonetheless usually have a sense that their attitude of maturity is an act put on for the benefit of others. When the act is accepted, these youths feel the therapist has been duped, much as their parents were; this only fuels the sense of omnipotence and eventually leads the patient to visit scorn and contempt upon the therapist.

An example of such a patient is Tina S., a 14-year-old girl hospitalized for being beyond parental control (part of this patient's treatment is reported in Sherwood 1990). An attractive, intelligent, and socially poised adolescent, Tina appeared far older than her age. She tended to treat peers and staff alike with an attitude of reserved interest and gave the clear impression of not needing others. Tina had long shown such a pseudomature facade. Her mother had been dependent on her and had not dared risking Tina's anger by frustrating her. In many ways she had been treated like an adult from an early age and had come to assume an adult's prerogatives. When these came by age 12 to include sexual activity, school refusal, and a variety of poorly controlled, potentially dangerous behaviors, her new stepfather tried to place limits on her. Tina was furious suddenly to be treated as a minor; a cycle of family fights began, ending in hospitalization after Tina physically attacked and injured her stepfather.

Tina is typical of out-of-control adolescents whose infantile omnipotence was not successfully challenged by their parents, who then sensed their parents' inability to master them, and who, out of the resulting disillusionment with their parents, resorted to a precocious self-sufficiency that masked general contempt for adults. In a latency-age child, this attitude may appear "cute," and the child may even be praised for his or her "maturity." However, adolescents who truly believe they are on equal footing with the adult world often come to behave in high-handed and poorly modulated ways. The adult world's restrictions on them as minors are experienced as narcissistic injuries; statutory offenses and potentially dangerous behavior then follow, eventually bringing the child into contact with a therapist or hospital.

Constitutional Factors Inhibiting Internalization

It has long been noted that children suffering from Attention Deficit Hyperactivity Disorder, learning disabilities, and other syndromes associated with that complex of problems that used to be referred to as Minimal Brain Dysfunction appear overrepresented among out-of-control youth (e.g., Hinshaw 1987, Shapiro and Garfinkel 1986, Stabenau 1984). In such cases constitutional factors may have prevented the child's submitting impulsivity and aggression to parental control. Neurological abnormalities may impair the capacity to internalize the values, standards, and expectations of the parents and other authorities. Such abnormalities appear to occur chiefly in the form of frontal lobe and left hemispheric syndromes and may interfere with development of the child's ability to regulate affect, take self as an object, and exercise volition (Joseph 1982, Miller 1988).

The result is that the growing child never fully cathects the external world, including the parents, and remains overly influenced by drive and impulse. In this case the struggle with the parents for control continues indefinitely, and the upsurge of instinctual energies that accompanies puberty heightens the child's feeling of power vis-à-vis parental control. The child is never fully enough controlled by the parents to envy their power and submit to it. Consequently, the denial of differences between the generations continues, and a healthy ego ideal is not formed.

Such individuals may seem insulated and terribly egocentric; the outside world is clearly less important to them than inner wishes and, in any event, external reality does not appear to have a lasting impact. These patients are often unduly fascinated with their own drives and impulses. They appear to notice how strong their urges and feelings are, and they seem impressed with this. One such patient repeatedly described how intensely and relentlessly angry he was, saying with evident pride, "I may be the kind of person who could kill someone without feeling nothin'!" This young man was inordinately impressed with the intensity of his anger, and he did not believe the outside world would be able to control or manage him. He said with a certain pleasure that he imagined he would have to be "locked up" to be controlled. This attitude is not unusual with this patient population. Inner urges are so overweening, and the external world seems so irrelevant, that the patient cannot experience inner urges with any perspective. Thus, there is an omnipotence about these patients: they experience their own inner impulses as the only relevant data, and, at most, the outside world seems to be something to react to, not something to which they must submit.

It would be easy to see these patients almost entirely in light of their undoubted biological etiology and to ignore the psychological factors. Treatment with psychostimulants or lithium appears to be the norm, and indeed these biological approaches may well help the patient focus on the outside world and/or manage aggression much more successfully (the patient just described responded well to lithium). All too often, the only psychological issues that are addressed are the patient's obvious social ineptness and learning problems. Of course these issues must be dealt with, but therapists should first address the ego ideal pathology that is also likely to be present. The ego ideal is the bridge by which children travel from the primacy of wish fulfillment and magical thinking to the larger world, where realistic accomplishments gradually build a base for pride and for attaining what is wanted. Attention Deficit Hyperactivity Disorder patients and other youth suffering related neurologically based syndromes, by contrast, have not had the means for building this bridge. The outside world has not seemed as important as their own hypercathected wishes.

Surprisingly, the clearest evidence of ego ideal pathology in these patients is their perfectionism. Once they start to put forth some effort at treatment, it usually becomes clear that these patients are intolerant of their own errors and terribly afraid of failing. At first glance, it may seem that they have internalized hypercritical parental attitudes and that these are behind their fear of failing. I believe, however, it is far more likely that perfectionism in this patient population reflects grandiosity, the patient's having remained his or her own ideal long past the oedipal stage. Essentially, these patients did not substitute realistic expectations and self-appraisals for omnipotent, magic-based thinking. They are afraid of failing because failure challenges their grandiosity.

Thus, therapists may confront ego ideal pathology in two forms when dealing with patients suffering Attention Deficit Hyperactivity Disorder and related syndromes. First, the child's inability to take the demands and standards of the outside world into account reflects a constitutionally based grandiosity—the child's own urges and impulses take precedence over parental wishes, and the child has never been made to envy adult prerogatives and submit to parental authority. Second, even when the patient is in fact trying to change, perfectionistic attitudes continue to show how much the child remains his or her own ideal.

Excessive Parental Sadism

A third source of disillusionment with adult authority, and one that usually leads to a different symptom picture, may be found when the rival parent *does* challenge the oedipal child's omnipotence but does so in a way that precludes identification with that parent. Freud (1923) described the identification that ends the oedipal struggle as a kind of submission to the authority of the father. In many cases, however, it may not be safe for the child to submit. If, for example, a father sadistically seeks to shame his son by displaying continual disappointment in him, or if the father is repeatedly violent with the son, then submission would come at the cost of feeling degraded and humiliated with nothing on which the child might rebuild pride. This situation tends to lead to ego ideal pathology, especially if the mother pursues a kind of clinging closeness with the boy. The mother's ongoing overinvestment in her son allows the child to perpetuate the fantasy of reunion with the primary love object in spite of the father's attempt to humble the child. The boy cannot identify with the father, and the mother's overinvestment offers a continuing basis for the pride that the father's harshness seeks to destroy. Thus, the child cannot afford to surrender the illusion of narcissistic perfection. The boy may well gain an understanding that the father is stronger (for the time being) but continues to feel he really can satisfy the mother's needs as well as the father's. In this case, not only is there no need to envy an adult, but it would be psychologically dangerous to do so, since envy would lead to a submission with no resulting identification.

When such children become symptomatic, they tend to engage in randomly destructive, impulsive, and aggressive forms of antisocial behavior, and they impress the therapist as being obnoxious, uncooperative, and oppositional from the beginning. It is tempting to conclude that the destructive behavior of these youths represents an identification with the sadism of the rival parent or an identification with the aggressor. I believe it is more likely, however, that no such identification has ever taken place and that the patient is expressing both fantasies of omnipotence (stemming from the illusion of being the admired and powerful infant of fusion) and also defiance against the authority of the sadistic father (and, by extension, all adult authority). What is completely lacking in such cases is any sense that there might be such a thing as a benevolent authority.

An example of such a case is a 20-year-old recovering addict in his second year of outpatient therapy after having undergone an inpatient chemical dependency treatment and having lived for a year at a halfway house. His inpatient treatment had followed four years of alcohol and drug abuse, frequent fights (many with his father), truancy and academic failure, and assorted illegal acts. His first year of outpatient treatment focused on his fear of women and on his discovery that he was terrified his mother would "take me over, like she did when I was a kid." In fact his mother had turned to him for her emotional life, largely with the consent of his abusive alcoholic father whose only involvement with his son was occasionally to show him "who's the boss." In the second year of therapy the patient began to have recurring dreams in which he was sexually involved with "another man's woman." In these dreams the other man would try to force the patient to perform fellatio on him, which simultaneously attracted and disgusted the patient. In daily life this patient was continually vigilant over whether his boss and other men were trying to "lord it over me." His dreams disappeared and he became more relaxed with adult men in general when he realized not only that the man in the dreams was his father, wanting him to submit, but also that his father had wanted submission for his own sadistic satisfaction, not for the purpose of giving his son any direction or identity.

In general the problem for these patients is the belief that all authorities want to humiliate them. Not surprisingly, there is a paranoid undercurrent to the clinical picture. These patients are bitter and cynical, and maintain with a nearly religious intensity the opinion that it is only a matter of time until everyone betrays them. This massive mistrust makes it impossible to give up their egocentricity, entitlement, and grandiosity, since in their experience submission equals degradation. They must remain impressed with themselves because they have no other source of pride.

This position makes it difficult for the patient to give up the oedipal denial of the differences between adults and children. When the patient has grown up with a sadistic parent, "adult" comes to equal "power," not moral authority. The exercise of power then seems purely arbitrary, carried out to dominate and humiliate, not for any overarching social purpose. Thus, adult simply means bigger and stronger, and there is no greater difference between children and adults than between smaller and larger children. It is difficult even to imagine what growing up might mean in this case; at most, the process of growing up means getting larger and more powerful, and eventually it means throwing one's strength around. Consequently, these are the patients most likely to engage in overtly antisocial behavior, as opposed to statutory offenses.

The Role of Sexual Abuse by an Adult

Those working with out-of-control adolescents may be surprised at the high percentage who were sexually abused while growing up. It is an easy (and undoubtedly correct) conclusion that such abuse must play a role in adolescent pathology. That conclusion is meaningless, however, if we fail to realize that the large and general category of sexual abuse covers a very wide spectrum of experiences, each of which carries its own consequences. It is my impression that many clinicians and hospitals routinely assign a Post-Traumatic Stress Disorder diagnosis to their patients who have suffered sexual abuse, which implies that trauma is seen as the chief problem. By focusing exclusively on trauma, however, clinicians virtually commit themselves to treating the patient as a victim, and issues of vulnerability, guilt, and catharsis automatically come to dominate treatment. With such a focus, the clinician may either fail to see narcissistic phenomena in the clinical picture altogether or assume that the patient's narcissistic features are reaction formations.

This is not to say that there is no trauma in sexual abuse. It is to say that the trauma is different for different types of abuse and that sometimes other features are more important than the traumatic features. If a patient was raped as a child, the trauma of violence is certainly likely to dominate the picture, and issues of vulnerability and physical integrity will eventually come to the forefront. If, however, a child is fondled or simply pursued sexually by a parent or other relative, or if the sexual experience was seductive, gentle, and affectionate, the results may be altogether different. In these cases narcissistic pathology rather than trauma may lie behind the symptom picture.

The narcissistic features in such a case come into clearer focus when we think the problem through from the standpoint of the ego ideal. The chief problem is that some types of abuse tend to perpetuate one of the two denials that are typical of the oedipal child, in this case denial of generational differences. If the child can serve as a sexual object for an adult, there is nothing an adult can do that a child cannot also do, and so there is no essential difference between children and adults except for size. The child can preserve (or recover) the illusion that he or she really could have satisfied the parent of the opposite sex. The oedipal illusion is maintained in such a case, and infantile grandiosity is not undermined—even if there is also an attendant sense of vulnerability, confusion, or outrage following the abuse.

The consequences for ego ideal formation are quite serious. A child who is allowed to remain his or her own ideal is turned in the wrong direction: the child does not point toward the future and toward gradually accomplishing those tasks that will bring independence and autonomy but toward the past and regression. In the case of female victims of sexual abuse, this regressive trend very often leads to sexual promiscuity. It has long been observed, in fact, that behaviorally disturbed boys tend to become aggressive while girls tend to become promiscuous.

This difference in symptoms reflects the difference between boys and girls vis-à-vis the primary love object, the mother. The oedipal boy must compete with the father for intimacy with his primary love object; insofar as he seeks to preserve the omnipotence of mother–infant fusion, he must usurp the father's place. By contrast, there is no such competition for the oedipal girl. Indeed, the opposite is true, since competition for the affection of the opposite sex parent threatens her closeness with the primary love object and signals that she is emotionally ready to risk losing closeness with the mother. Consequently, the boy engages in the oedipal struggle to *avoid* growing up, while the girl presses it when she is *ready* to begin growing up. The oedipal girl's way of expressing the regressive drive for mother–infant fusion is to yearn for her own baby in order to identify with her child and enjoy vicariously her baby's omnipotence. To the extent that the girl seeks a return to the perfection of mother–infant fusion, she does not want to have the father but to have his baby. Consequently, adolescent girls are inclined toward promiscuity when sexual abuse leads to ego ideal pathology.

Thus, female patients who have been sexually abused by an adult will tend to be sexually promiscuous. The abuse strengthened their denial of the difference between adults and children, thereby interfering with their ability to resolve the oedipal struggle and form a healthy ego ideal. As a result, they entered adolescence with infantile omnipotence intact and sought behaviors that expressed the desire for a return to the perfection of mother–infant fusion. Sexual behavior is the most obvious expression of that desire, representing the wish for a baby with whom the patient can identify. As long as the patient continues to deny the difference between adults and children, regressive behaviors will also continue.

A further consequence of sexual abuse, and one that also contributes to ego ideal pathology, is that the image of adults is compromised. When adults relate to the children in their lives as sexual objects, they make it impossible for the child to idealize them and imply to the child that relationships are exploitative and based on need satisfaction or tension reduction. These implications have a leveling effect, negating the difference between adults and children and thereby preserving or reviving the child's oedipal denial. These parents cannot challenge the child's natural narcissism; the child cannot project grandiosity onto such a parent nor can that parent become a model. Rather, the child is fixed in a pattern of regressive, infantile relationships, in which attachments are built on need rather than affection and responsibility.

If the ego ideal is, as Chasseguet-Smirgel (1985) suggests, the tool by which the child embraces the idea of *development*, then the sexually abused child stays in a static world where development is not needed. The idea of development is that competencies, abilities, and accomplishments lead the child into the future. If, however, relationships are built on need satisfaction, no development needs to occur. In such a case, instinct (drive, wish, desire) is all that matters, and this already exists without development. The child is taught by the sexually abusing adult that he or she already has all that is necessary for filling an adult role, and development is simply something that occurs biologically (that is, with one's body), not with one's self. If development is purely physical, one may become more (or possibly less) desirable but not different. Time becomes static, not a progression forward or toward a not-yet-known future: the future *is* known; it is the same as the present, and therefore development need not occur and indeed has no meaning.

The sexually abused child who goes on to become an out-of-control adolescent expresses his or her indifference to development in a variety of ways. There is a surprising degree of academic failure among such youth, and this suggests a latent sense that there is nothing really to prepare for, that the future brings no challenge not already contained in the present. Similarly, these youths tend to take many chances and place themselves in dangerous circumstances. It is not unusual, for instance, for sexually abused girls to place themselves in vulnerable situations and be raped as adolescents. They seem not to anticipate that such a thing could occur even though an outside observer may not see how they could be so blind. It is tempting to conclude that they place themselves in a position to be taken advantage of as a repetition compulsion, but it is more likely, I think, that the adolescent who was sexually abused does not yet believe in cause-and-effect reality. These youths still live in the grandiose world of magic and wish fulfillment. They can therefore make themselves believe that no danger exists if they do not want to see it.

EGO IDEAL PATHOLOGY AND THE FORM OF RESISTANCE

There may be some rough correlation between the type of ego ideal pathology an adolescent shows and the form of resistance that will be evident in treatment. In general, patients whose parents were reluctant to win the oedipal struggle tend to show narcissistic resistance. In effect, these parents trained the child to feel in charge and superior, and this is the patient's later style with the therapist. It has also been my experience that patients showing constitutional factors that inhibit internalization also show narcissistic forms of resistance. In addition, excessive parental sadism tends to lead to paranoid and schizoid forms of resistance. Finally, sexual abuse seems to be associated with affective lability or with paranoid resistance.

These correlations, however, are very rough indeed. Therapists should not count on being able to deduce the precise type of ego ideal pathology from the form of resistance being shown. To begin with, there are many exceptions to these correlations. Further, out-of-control patients can often shift from one form of resistance to another, and in such a case the therapist will not know which pattern of resistance is the one associated with the underlying ego ideal pathology.

EGO IDEAL PATHOLOGY AND AGE-APPROPRIATE DEVELOPMENTAL ISSUES

In Chapter 2 I argued that age-appropriate developmental issues were not crucial factors in the resistance showed by out-of-control adolescents, and I suggested that this was because these patients are turned backwards, so to speak, pursuing infantile aims and, if anything, trying to avoid age-appropriate tasks. If the (more or less) normal adolescent is trying to break away from the parents and avoid the incestuous implications of needing the parent of the opposite sex, this is not a major concern for the out-of-control patient. These patients, by contrast, seek a return to the world of mother and infant, trying to preserve the illusion of being the admired infant of fusion, caught in the admiring gaze of the mother.

This is not to say that all out-of-control adolescents are close to their mothers, although a surprising number of them are. It is to say two things. First, these patients are almost always caught up in very intense struggles with their parents. Both they and the parents tend to cling to these struggles even though they entail very painful and difficult battles. The key to understanding the fact that neither patient nor parent seems quite willing to avoid these battles by doing things differently is that the intensity of the struggle is itself a form of fused relatedness. Patients may recover the illusion of fusion through battles that are intense and prolonged enough to break down separateness and boundaries. Consequently, they may *seem* to be fighting, but in reality they are grasping after powerfully charged interactions that ultimately offer the satisfaction of oneness.

Second, even if the out-of-control adolescent pushes a parent away, the parent may be replaced by a new relationship that offers the same dynamics. A male patient may reject or fight off his mother only to seek a girlfriend who mothers and admires him, thereby recovering the sense of being his own ideal. In this case nothing has really changed except the cast of characters. Female patients may push away their parents but wind up with dating relationships in which they are treated as infants. They are not seen by their boyfriends as being separate persons and are perpetually reduced to helpless, needy status. Eventually it becomes clear that they want to be taken care of (rather than cared for) and do this by repeatedly becoming helpless—sometimes threatening self-harm in order to coerce caretaking. In this case the girl has not really moved away from the family; she is still dealt with as a child and, if anything, is even further away from autonomy.

We will miss the ego ideal pathology that underlies the out-of-control patient's overt symptoms if we assume that they, like most adolescents, are trying to establish separate identities or pursue other age-appropriate tasks. In general, they are not. They are, rather, trying to recover or preserve a world in which they are their own ideals or in which they may identify with someone who can fill the role. Out-of-control adolescents are turned in the wrong direction, pursuing the past rather than the future.

CHAPTER 4

NARCISSISTIC RESISTANCE

VALUE, DEVALUATION, AND REALITY

Grunberger (1989) has said that narcissism is a matter of value. If this is true, the therapist may understand much of what happens with the patient engaged in narcissistic resistance as an effort to sustain the illusion of having great value. The patient may try to use the therapist in this project. The therapist is dehumanized or depersonified—as are most persons in the narcissistic patient's life—and is reduced to the status of a mirror for the patient. The therapist is experienced as someone who has value only to the extent that he or she can confirm the patient's self-valuation by reflecting the desired image back to the patient. The patient's interest is not in the actual therapist but only in the therapist as an extension of the patient's illusions of value.

Of course, these things are truly illusory. Adolescent patients engaged in narcissistic resistance have not built self-valuation on actual accomplishments and in fact usually have rather fewer accomplishments than others their age. They are not, therefore, looking for what is often termed *mirroring* in the literature, even if they use the therapist as a mirror. Indeed, an accurate and empathic reflection is not likely to be welcomed or even heard. They want their mirrors to sustain their illusions of value. In practical terms this means that adolescent narcissistic patients put a certain pressure on therapists to like and enjoy them, take their side against their parents, and overvalue their occasional accomplishments.

It is well known that narcissistic injuries evoke anger or even outrage in most people. This is certainly true with adolescent patients. Therapists who fail to sustain the patient's narcissistic illusions can expect to be angrily devalued, which is the patient's attempt to cloud the mirror, as Grunberger (1989) put it. By devaluing the therapist, the patient renders the therapist's opinions irrelevant and harmless. If the patient were to argue about it, try to understand the therapist's point of view, or attempt to correct deficiencies spotted by the therapist, the narcissistic illusion of value would be lost. By doing any of these things, the patient would have entered into a relationship with external reality and would be struggling with reality to forge an image of the self. But this is not part of the narcissistic program. External reality, the locus of the narcissistic wound, is simply denied, not wrestled with, and the therapist, the agent of external reality, is devalued.

The devaluation is an attempt to destroy reality and preserve the child's world of magic and illusion. Knowing this gives the therapist an insight into the world in which the patient lives and also into the patient's likely response to the therapist. The patient, trying to cloud the mirror, will devalue the therapist more or less vehemently. The patient will try to sustain a sense of not needing the therapist and being self-sufficient. This can be done by distance or by anger. If patients try to create distance, they will be aloof and will support the aloofness through contempt and disdain. If they become angry, they will use the anger to create a barrier or wall. In either case the therapist may feel dismissed and discounted.

Therapists may be tempted try to counter narcissistic resistance through confrontation (e.g., Langs 1974b), a basic therapeutic intervention that is, in essence, any correction of a reality distortion (Langs 1974a). This intervention will not, however, be successful. The patient will not respond to the idea that he or she is at odds with reality precisely because the patient is engaged in a thoroughgoing denial and avoidance of that reality. It is therefore irrelevant to the patient that there is some conflict with reality. As long as the magical illusion of value is intact, reality is something that can be dismissed or experienced in a distorted manner.

There are several elements to the patient's denial of ordinary reality. These include: the refusal to accept cause-and-effect sequences, the attendant loss of the sense of agency, the inability to see authority as anything more than a matter of power, and the experience of time as a series of disconnected instants.

The Denial of Cause-and-Effect Reality

Most persons experience what happens as part of a sequence in which one set of events leads to new events in a way that is more or less predictable or at least understandable. However, those patients operating out of a narcissistic orientation do not fully see the relationship between what they do and what consequently happens. Such a relationship can be accepted only if the *impersonal* nature of events is also accepted. Cause-and-effect sequences obtain independent of what we want; they unfold according to indifferent and impersonal laws once a certain series of events is set in motion. The narcissistic adolescent has not been able to accept an experience of the world as something that unfolds with indifference to his or her wishes. Consequently, the narcissistic patient can want and demand, but it is difficult for such a person to take meaningful, planned action, particularly if the action entails delaying gratification.

Action implies that events are independent of our wishes, that "wishing won't make it so," and this is an implication the narcissistic individual cannot accept. Determined, purposeful action feels alien to the patient who demands that events turn on his or her wishes and wants. Wishes form a magical connection with the world, a connection that is broken if some more chancy and mediated step—in this case, action—must be taken. While determined action may feel highly personal to the mature individual, it feels unsatisfying and offensive to the narcissistic person. Indeed, it is a source of frustration and a narcissistic wound to believe that planning and work are required; to the narcissistic mentality, demands should be enough.

In such a world, causality—as opposed to magic and omnipotence—comes from outside the self (Bach 1985). Contingency is an unwelcome idea, since contingency implies that the individual is not the center of events and that other factors than wants must be reckoned with. Thus contingency feels somehow annoying and unfair and is an insult to the patient's grandiosity. The narcissistic mentality tries to keep these sullying influences away from the grandiose and overvalued view of the self. Consequently, whatever happens by contingency is experienced as alien to oneself, as taking place away from and external to the self. Whatever happens that the narcissistic patient did not wish to happen must be accounted for through reference to other people or blind luck.

Narcissistic adolescents are therefore unable to experience responsibility for what they do or for the predicaments in which they find themselves. Similarly they are surprisingly unable to achieve even simple plans of action. They may intellectually see the need to study, for instance, and may force themselves to do this for periods of time. But they cannot sustain the effort; it offends their view of themselves, and they frequently make good beginnings only to fail to follow through. Their experience of the inevitably disappointing results is that others did not do their part or that their luck turned bad. They simply cannot surrender to the idea that the world operates independent of themselves (and that they therefore must take purposeful action), since this would mean that they are not the center of what happens.

> This tendency to blame luck or ill will can take on an almost comic aspect, as with an adolescent who broke into the police chief's house, vandalized it, got drunk on the chief's liquor, and was found throwing up in his pool by officers. When the young man was subsequently sent to long-term treatment, the staff asked him if he could see what he had done to get sent there. He repeatedly insisted, "I didn't do nothin', man. It was just bad luck—that police chief had it in for me, I guess."

The Absence of the Sense of Agency

If one lives in a world in which events are matters of wishes and/or luck, there is no sense of being the author of one's life and deeds. There is no experience of being able to stand within the swirl of competing cause–effect sequences, impacting the world through purposeful action. Most of us would agree, of course, that there is some disquieting measure of luck in whatever we accomplish (or fail to accomplish), but it is one factor among others for most persons, who feel that, along with luck, their own preparation, intentionality, and actions create much of what happens in their lives. It is possible that this is an illusion but, if it is, it is a necessary illusion. How painful is its absence can be seen in the distress of individuals whose lives are taking turns beyond their personal control, such as those who are terminally ill or those who are suddenly left by a spouse.

Narcissistic adolescents, by contrast, stand to the side of their own lives, experiencing pleasure and frustration at what occurs but not ownership. As already mentioned, this precludes any sense of responsibility and also any deep sense of guilt or remorse or, for that matter, pride. It may seem odd to say that these individuals do not feel pride, since they can be among the most arrogant of creatures. Their pride, however, is founded on infantile entitlement and demandingness, not on realistic accomplishments. They therefore feel no more proud when something goes as they wish than they had felt before. Healthy pride is based on a sense of competence and effectuality, on the experience of making the desired impact on the world. For the narcissistic individual, however, even the idea of having to impact the world is ego-dystonic, since this implies that the world is separate from the individual's wishes. The narcissistic adolescent, therefore, does not experience the self as a center of autonomy and initiative (Kohut 1971). The self is more the passive recipient of what happens, inflating and deflating as the world is congruent or discordant with the narcissist's demands.

The absence of agency interferes with the therapist's use of conventional interventions. It is useless to point out that the patient's expectations are unrealistic, that behavior did not match up with reality, or that self-perceptions are not built on reality if the patient has no sense of being the author of these things (Miller 1986). At best the therapist will seem to the patient to misunderstand the matter completely, since these patients will not feel that they had a direct and purposeful hand in what happened. Patients will wonder why the therapist is blaming them for what others did to them or for their own unfortunate luck. At worst, such patients will assume that the therapist envies them and is putting them down for that reason. In neither case can the narcissistic patient learn from interventions that presuppose a conventional sense of ownership of one's life and actions.

The Narcissistic Experience of Authority

The narcissistic adolescent denies the difference between adults and children, as outlined in Chapter 3. As one drug-dealing, 16-year-old said, "Adults and children: I like to think we're all the same really." Adults are simply seen as larger and having more options than children or youth, but not as essentially different. The key variable is *power*. For the narcissistic adolescent, adulthood, and by implication authority, is a matter of having more power. The only point in growing up is accordingly not to gain in competence and maturity but, rather, to become more powerful, to be in a position to do what one wants and make others respond to one's demands. Growing up, therefore, is purely chronological; there is no psychological progression attached to the concept. Growing up is only gaining physical prowess and political rights.

In such a state of mind, rules and limits appear to be utterly arbitrary. If authority is a matter only of power, then the rules dictated by authority are experienced as designed to safeguard that power. They are not seen as having anything to do with the common good, with tradition or community, or as coming out of collective wisdom. Rather, they are viewed as bald-faced attempts to keep those who have less power in a subservient posture.

When the rules are seen as arbitrary, the only reason to follow them is if the other has enough power to make one do so. Once it dawns on the narcissistically oriented adolescent that the parents do not have the means, or perhaps the will, to enforce rules, there is little reason to comply. Compliance is likely to be something that occurs episodically, lulling the family into periods of feeling that matters have gotten better. They have not, however. Once the patient is upset enough or wants something enough, the rules will again be violated. And why not? From the patient's perspective, the parents lost most of their power once the child gained physical maturity. It is often the case that the only thing that will renew compliance is a willingness by the parents to have a physical confrontation. While this may bring a new period of compliance, it only reinforces the patient's sense that adulthood is indeed a matter of having more power.

It has been widely observed that the therapist will be experienced as an extension of the adults in the patient's life (Aarons 1970, Deutsch 1944, Geleerd 1957, Katan 1935). This is true enough but not in the way usually meant. The patient is not simply transferring age-appropriate developmental issues from the parents to the person of the therapist. That transference will be buried under the patient's general denial of the difference between adults and children. Consequently, this expected transference reaction is not accessible during the resistance stage of treatment. Rather, the patient will view the therapist as yet another adult intent on preserving power against the adolescent's wishes to gain equality.

The narcissistic adolescent will enter therapy prepared to hear anything challenging or critical as an expression of the therapist's desire to keep the patient under adult control. Confrontations and even relatively mild questions cannot be heard as the therapist intends them, therefore, and may draw unexpected antagonism. The therapist will be viewed as someone hired to do the parents' or the court's bidding, intent presumably on delaying the patient's access to adult prerogatives. This is a serious distortion of the therapist's communications and means that the therapist will at the very best have trouble getting the patient to accept even the most mild observations about problematic behaviors or attitudes.

The Experience of Time

Time does not flow for the narcissistically disturbed adolescent. It consists of disconnected moments of excitement and energy followed by periods of boredom and ennui that are experienced as unrelated to what came before. Moments of excitement or boredom may last for minutes or for days or even weeks. The duration is not actual clock time but purely subjective. These periods (of excitement or boredom) are defined by the moment's affective valence; as long as the excitement (or boredom) lasts, the moment lasts and then ends, to be followed by a new moment with a new valence.

There can be no more sequential or continuous experience of time because there is no more continuous experience of the self. If there is no sense of agency, there is no sense of the self's continuing across different events and circumstances. Thus, the experience of time is not like a movie but more like a group of still pictures. In turn, this discontinuous view of time interferes with any attempt to acquaint the patient with cause–effect sequences. The patient seeks to attain moments of pleasurable excitement during which the self can be inflated and the illusion sustained that the world orbits around the patient. Of course, this makes it hard for the patient to maintain any commitments or to take planful action that might lead to the experience of mastery or competence.

The patient's choppy view of time can often be seen in daily life. Many narcissistic patients have trouble keeping a job or staying with such commitments as sports. Even when they successfully engage in such activities, one hears employers or coaches complain that the patient is not putting forth full effort, or that the patient is very hard to motivate. It is common to hear that the patient has lost several apparently easy jobs or that he or she has lost interest in a sports activity that was seemingly important earlier in life. These reports underscore the narcissistic patient's inability to generate a *lasting* interest in anything. Activities are valued momentarily, but when excitement is not available the moment is over, followed by boredom. It is not usually helpful to show the patient the connection between sustained effort and good results at work or in sports. The patient is not thinking of time as a flowing sequence in which tedious and boring work may lead to gratification later. Rather, the patient cannot connect the tedious period of preparation with the final accomplishment. Each appears to be a disconnected moment with no necessary relation between them.

The therapy session itself will be one such moment, usually a period of boredom or tedium. The patient may intellectually be able to remember what was done in previous sessions, but it will be very hard to experience any actual continuity between what came before and the current session. Generally the patient will experience a session almost entirely in terms of whether it is exciting or gratifying. The therapist's version of a good session is therefore quite different from the patient's version.

OBJECT RELATIONS, EGOCENTRICITY, AND THE FAILURE OF EMPATHY

To the extent narcissism is indeed a matter of valuation (Grunberger 1989), others are seen in terms of their ability to sustain the illusion of overvaluation. The fulcrum on which this aspect of the narcissistic adolescent's relations with others turns is *egocentricity*, or the tendency to see events purely from one's own, immediate point of view. The narcissistic adolescent cannot endorse—and sometimes cannot even see—alternate points of view. Indeed, alternative perspectives may even be experienced as a narcissistic injury or as a challenge to the patient's grandiosity. Consequently, any difference between the patient and another person is at best met with indifference and, more typically, is felt to be an annoyance or cause of frustration. The patient seeks relationships in which the other person is an extension of the self, relationships in which others revolve around the patient's orbit.

It is possible that the narcissistic adolescent will admire another person, perhaps for that individual's beauty, style, or power. In such a case, the patient may be willing to be an extension of the other and will feel valued by being in orbit around an exciting, admirable other. But this is not really a change in interpersonal relations. In either case the pattern of relationships is such that a kind of oneness is sought and differences are not tolerated. At the center of a relationship is one person, whose admirable and exciting traits dominate the picture with others serving merely as planets revolving around the central person's sun. Thus, the narcissistic adolescent may become attached to a gang leader, for instance, or may come to idealize a powerful staff on an inpatient unit (Aichhorn 1964, Eissler 1950). This central person is the source of value, with the others basking in a kind of reflected glory; it is still the world of the Ideal.

Narcissistic egocentricity constitutes what almost amounts to a thought disorder (cf. Bach 1985). Events are experienced from such a thoroughgoing self-referential perspective that anything that fails to fit is either not seen at all or discounted immediately. The result is a very narrow view of events, one that is too narrow in fact to be realistic. Too much is being ignored or tuned out and too much is being interpreted solely in terms of the patient's self-interest. The consequent experience of others is very highly personalized, so personalized that it is impossible for the patient to see the self as one center of meaning among many others. In short, all of the world that falls outside of the patient's own wishes is ignored.

Friendships are not built on attachment or affection in such a world but on the extent to which another person fits in with the patient's wishes. Typically, those who use drugs or take part in other activities with the patient are valued. Those who are different are discounted or actively attacked. In a successful treatment, these patients may suddenly realize that they were used by their "friends" and also that they did the same thing. Patients are sometimes shocked to find this out. At the time they never regarded such behavior as anything more than what friends do with each other.

It is easy to see how such limited relationships can be confused with friendship when we consider that the narcissistic patient is not able to empathize. Egocentricity means that the patient cannot assume the other person's point of view or temporarily identify with the other (empathy). Rather, the patient merely assumes that the other's perspective is identical with the patient's. Needless to say, the other person is not known or understood but simply confused with the patient. In such a world, relationships typically do not last. It is not usual for narcissistic patients to have long-lasting friendships unless they involve drug use. Such use of drugs may form a basis for a sustained relationship because the experience of getting high together may obliterate boundaries and thereby sustain the illusion that there are no real differences.

Therapists often express surprise at the coldness and ruthlessness that narcissistic adolescents direct at their parents. Indeed, parents sometimes bring their adolescents for treatment after an encounter that reveals these traits. The parents are stunned to find that the patient appears to have no interest in the family nor in the parents' wishes and feelings. To the extent that the patient experiences the world from a narcissistic state of mind, this is true, of course: there is no room for love in narcissism, only for valuation, which is defined egocentrically. It is true these patients often show an intense involvement with family members, usually the mother. It can seem to be the case that every interaction is supercharged with strong affect, suggesting that family members are not emotionally separate from one another. This lack of separateness is not love, however. Such interactions are regressive in nature; they aim to deny differentiation and to support the world of the Ideal.

The therapist, therefore, can be excused for not quite knowing how to break into the patient's world. Certainly the patient will not be especially interested in the therapist or in anything the therapist might have to say that is beyond the bounds of whatever is of immediate interest to the patient, nor will the patient feel motivated to work out of loyalty to the family or from a sense of remorse for how others have been treated. Self-interest rules the situation. If the patient is already in control of what is happening at home, there is little reason for the patient to change; the patient will simply want others to change. The patient's egocentricity really allows no other stance.

THE TREATMENT OF OVERVALUATION
OF THE SELF AND EGOCENTRICITY

The problem for the therapist is how to break into such a self-contained system. The parents or the courts may be able to force the patient to attend sessions, but it is of course a rather different matter to make something happen there that is therapeutic. An approach, however, may be fashioned using Leary's (1957) ideas, outlined in Chapter 1. We recall that Leary suggested that behavior seldom takes place in an interpersonal vacuum, that what we do is generally intended (consciously or unconsciously) to pull a certain attitude or type of response from the other person. To the extent the other reacts as we intend, the interaction is comfortable, even if it is characterized by tension or anger. To the extent the other person responds differently than what our behavior is intended to pull, we will be uneasy with the exchange.

If we also remember the principle from Chapter 1 that therapy takes place when the therapist becomes a problem for the patient (the solving of which forces the patient to wrestle with his or her pathology), we may begin to build a therapeutic response to the problems posed by the narcissistic adolescent. The chief problem is the patient's insulation from us, the utter self-sufficiency of the narcissistic program. The therapist must build a pattern of interaction that gains some foothold in that world and then disrupts it, driving the patient to patterns of interaction that are incompatible with his or her grandiosity and egocentricity. It is a matter of moving the patient out of his or her comfort zone.

This is done, in effect, by delivering a certain type of narcissistic injury. It may sound strange to propose that narcissistic resistance is to be treated with a narcissistic wound, but we must remember that this is essentially how life moves all of us beyond the natural megalomania of childhood (see Chapter 3 for a fuller discussion of the process). In normal development parents "engage with and appropriately discipline the children's narcissism" (Rinsley 1982, p. 193) as they gradually require more and more conformity from the child and demand the attainment of competencies that later life will require. When infantile megalomania is confronted with parental standards and limits, there is unavoidable—but ultimately benevolent—pain and humiliation for the child. There is a naturally occurring and necessary narcissistic injury as the child learns that his or her own wishes must be exchanged for what the adult world expects. This is the humiliation of being treated like a child. As Cameron (1963) said, "No matter what they have thought, and no matter what people tell them, they are not little men or little women but little children" (p. 74).

When this benevolent humiliation does not take place in the course of the patient's development, it must take place in therapy. Confronted with an adolescent showing narcissistic resistance, the therapist must find ways to inflict the narcissistic wound that will propel the patient away from egocentricity and grandiosity and toward the larger world. In a sense, the therapist is trying to acquaint the patient with external reality, with the unwelcome idea that there are limits and laws that will not yield to the patient's wishes and that will ultimately speak to the patient in the hard language of facts. No matter what the individual's age, this lesson is never an easy one; when it must be learned in adolescence, it is of necessity unpleasant for the patient.

There are three steps to the process of inflicting this benevolent narcissistic injury. First, therapists must show that they are a different sort of authority figure, namely, authorities who are not uneasy with the patient's rebellious or antisocial wishes. Second, the therapist must assume a narcissistic posture, using that stance to deflate the patient's grandiosity. Finally, the therapist must handle the patient's distress and anger, gradually moving toward a less narcissistic posture. Each stage will be discussed in turn.

Being a Different Kind of Authority

This is the therapist's first opportunity to violate the patient's expectations. The patient is prepared to see the therapist as a representative of the parents' world, as an authority figure, albeit an authority without much power. Given the way the narcissistic patient defines authority, the therapist will be expected to be interested chiefly in compliance or conventionality. Even if superficial compliance is offered initially, the narcissistic patient is contemptuous of the therapist's presumed conventionality. From this position, the therapist has little impact on the patient. It is therefore important for the therapist to be seen as someone who can identify with the patient's contempt and defiance (Noshpitz 1957, Sherwood 1990).

Therapists must not try to identify with the patient by showing that they are like the patient but, rather, by assuming the role of one who can judge the value of the patient's defiance and contempt. As noted in Chapter 1, therapists all too often try to forge a relationship by renouncing their membership in the adult world and telling the patient, in one way or another, that they themselves are really adolescents at heart. This amounts to trying to pursue or seduce the patient into treatment, a strategy that cannot succeed. It leaves the therapist no room to become a representative of reality later in the treatment, which is the stance the therapist must eventually assume if narcissistic resistance is to be ended. The therapist's best position is to demonstrate a sympathetic understanding of the patient's motives and behavior while at the same time taking the role of critic, of someone who can pass judgment on the adequacy of what the patient did.

Therapists must show that they are not shocked or offended by the patient's behavior but are not much impressed either. To accomplish this, therapists must let loose of their own conventionality, establishing themselves as persons who might harbor a few narcissistic or antisocial intentions of their own and who might therefore have some sympathy with the patient's viewpoint. At the same time, however, the therapist reserves the right to pass judgment on how well or how intelligently the patient acted. The therapist must communicate familiarity with the patient's territory and imply that he or she is much more a master of that territory than the patient is.

> One narcissistic patient began his first session by saying, "This [therapy] is such a scam. Don't you feel guilty when you go home at night for taking money for this?" The therapist replied, "Only people who have to work hard go home from the office at night. I prefer not to have to work that hard. I always leave early, in the afternoon at the latest." The patient was visibly surprised, having assumed that the therapist would be offended at the idea he was a con artist and would defend himself.

> Another patient in a residential treatment center tried to put the therapist on the defensive in his first group therapy session. He accused the therapist and other staff of not caring about him and being in it only for the money, an approach that had placed staff on the defensive at another facility. He appeared taken aback when the therapist replied that he thought there was considerable financial value to the patient but could not say yet whether there was any other value to him and therefore could not say whether the pa-

tient was worth caring about. He then outlined the center's per diem charges under the patient's contract and added up the total money the staff could expect to receive for each month the patient was with them. He finally encouraged the patient to continue resisting treatment, since that would make it easier to justify a lengthy and more profitable stay.

Being able to adopt the patient's own narcissistic stance need not always be abrasive or antagonistic. Therapists can simply display sympathy with the patient's apparent motives or offer suggestions on how the patient could have accomplished presumed goals more effectively. If therapists believe the patient's parents have handled a situation poorly, this can be said aloud along with the conclusion, "I'm not sure they gave you much reason to do differently" or "I wouldn't want people like that telling me what to do either." If a patient has done something creative or clever, therapists should go out of their way to show delight at these traits. The goal is to show that the patient's behavior is not alarming or shocking and, if possible, to enjoy the patient.

Therapists will have to prepare the patient's family for this approach. Narcissistic adolescents will want to get out of therapy or at the very least use the therapist against the parents. They can be counted on to bring to the parents' attention anything said in a session that might offend or bother anyone in the family. Whenever therapists make a derogatory comment about the parents or appear to agree with the patient's motives, it will almost certainly get back to the family. There will be no "honor among thieves" with a narcissistic adolescent.

The therapist must make a judgment call on the extent to which parents can understand the therapeutic intent behind comments that sound antisocial or critical. Often parents can understand what the therapist is trying to accomplish and tolerate it, especially if they are coached on how to react when the patient tries to play therapist and parents against each other. In such a case, the therapist should tell the parents what to expect, predicting the patient's attempt to upset the parents with some unflattering remark by the therapist. The parents can be coached to react by saying it is clear the patient is trying to drive a wedge between them and the therapist and that this won't work. The parents may also be urged to agree with any criticism of them that the patient may report; whenever the parents can do this, the therapist will gain status in the patient's eyes.

Unhappily, it is often obvious that the parents will not be able to tolerate any comment that implies criticism or is at odds with how they see matters. When this is the case, therapists must choose their words more carefully. Even so, it is usually possible to find comments to make that will communicate to the patient that the therapist is more comfortable than most adults with the patient's contempt and defiance and that the therapist can even enjoy some of the patient's liveliness, cleverness, or stubbornness.

Once such a comment is made, it should not be pursued. If the therapist tries to emphasize the point, the patient will feel that he or she is being seduced or that it is important to the therapist to be acceptable to the patient. This is not, of course, what the therapist wants. By contrast, the therapist is simply trying to demonstrate an ability to identify with the patient while at the same time withholding any endorsement. The therapist seeks to be a different sort of authority from what the patient expects, one who is easy with the patient's behavior and motives but who could probably have accomplished the patient's apparent goals better than the patient did.

One patient described sneaking out of the house, stealing his father's car, and partying all night. He did this after his father set what he thought were unfair limits on going out at night. The patient had gotten caught and was brought to therapy. The therapist said that the patient had handled matters badly and should be able to do better. The patient replied that he supposed the therapist would have played by the rules, to which the therapist replied that he would have done so only if it would have gotten him what he wanted but that in any event he would have been much smarter than to have gotten caught at whatever he decided to do. He seemed to catch the patient off guard by asking why he was so clumsy as to get caught. The therapist then declared that the goal of therapy would be making the patient smart enough to get what he wanted without paying an unacceptable price.

One 16-year-old girl was brought to therapy by her mother with the threat that she would be sent to long-term treatment if therapy did not succeed. The therapist suggested to the patient that he could help her learn to manipulate her mother so that she did not have to go to "one of those awful places." Happily, the patient did not seem to notice that the therapist's idea of manipulating the mother was terribly close to having the patient follow the mother's rules. When the patient had conflicts with the mother, the therapist took care to reframe the situation. For instance, he would accuse the patient of "doing a bad job of manipulating" whenever the patient broke a rule and repeatedly advised, "Never get in a fight you can't win with your mother." The patient seemed willing to hear and follow the therapist's advice when it was put in such terms. She could not have done so had the therapist not cast his remarks in anti-social language.

This approach places a strain on the therapist. It requires some ability to endorse defiant, sneaky, stubborn behavior and motives. The risk is that the therapist may not be fully in control of his or her own antisocial tendencies and may act out such tendencies through the patient. Consequently, the therapist *must* remain able to step back from the situation and understand the motives for taking this approach. One of the things of which the therapist must stay aware is that there is in fact an antisocial motive involved: the therapist is not being honest and is indeed manipulating the patient under the guise of being able to identify with the patient's defiance. Such a motive is inherently aggressive in nature, and therapists may feel some discomfort with this. To succeed in this first step, therapists must be able to meet narcissistic patients on their own terms, entering into their world and sharing at least for a time their grandiosity and omnipotence.

Deflating the Patient's Grandiosity

This step begins when the therapist decides to inflict a narcissistic injury, aimed at the patient's grandiosity. If all goes well, the therapist will not need to take this second step until the first step is in place, that is, until the patient has come to see the therapist as someone who is not alarmed or offended by the patient's grandiosity and defiance. It is often the case that all does not go well, and therapists may find that they must move to the second step unsure of how the patient sees them or unsure that the patient views them as different sorts of authorities from what the patient expected. It is my experience that treatment goes better if the first step can be taken, but it is the second step that is crucial.

Possible Interventions

When therapists are ready to move to the second step, they must begin to fall silent during the session. This is a change, and the way can be prepared by saying to the patient something to the effect, "Well, we've gotten a feel for one another now. It's time to do some work. What do you want to work on?" This preparatory remark in itself contains a narcissistic wound, since it implies that the therapist sees the patient as someone who needs help or has something to learn. These implications also imply a generational boundary, that the patient is the therapist's junior.

After making such preparatory remarks, the therapist should become silent and largely unresponsive. It is not likely that the patient will respond with a request for help from the therapist or with a theme that is indeed therapeutically relevant. It is more likely that the patient will be confused or offended by the therapist's silence. Grandiose people do not enjoy not being responded to.

The immediate result is tension in the session. This is a good sign, since the tension means that the therapist is becoming a problem for the patient's grandiosity. The fact that the therapist is not reacting means that the patient does not control the therapist, which in turn implies that the therapist is different from the patient, rather than an extension of the patient. Silence implies a world of differentiation that is an offense to the patient's desire for a seamless universe of which he or she is the center. The silence suggests that the therapist can resist the patient, that the therapist can do without the patient.

The therapist's silence also implies criticism of the patient. If narcissism is a matter of valuation, the therapist's silence is devaluing. In the first stage of work with the narcissistic adolescent, the therapist tried to assume the posture of someone who could make judgments about the patient and who might enjoy the patient but who would not be impressed. This stance contributes to the impact of the therapist's silence, which will very likely be experienced as negative or critical by the patient. At the very least, the silence will feel like a demand that the therapist is suddenly placing on the patient.

The therapist ought not, therefore, be concerned if the patient seems upset. This is in fact precisely what the therapist wants, and the therapist should be concerned if the patient is *not* upset. As noted earlier, most persons are upset by narcissistic injuries, and this is what the therapist's silence is intended to be. Most narcissistic adolescents will be angered by the silence, while others will be confused and subdued. The atmosphere of the session is sure to become troubled in some way if the intervention has its desired effect.

The therapist should not stop here but should look for ways to increase the tension level. Specifically, the therapist should define the patient's reaction to the silence as inadequate. This may be done by remaining silent when the patient asks questions or by making comments that are designed to raise tension.

One 17-year-old was agitated when, in their fifth session, his therapist first asked him to start working on more important issues and then fell totally silent. He began demanding to know why the therapist was so quiet but received no reply. The therapist was quiet, though attentive, until late in the session when he finally answered the patient's question about his silence by replying, "So far you've not said anything worth responding to." The patient looked utterly surprised and did not know what to say. It was clearly something he was not prepared for, and he was terribly angry. However, several months later he remembered this comment as "the thing that really got me going in treatment."

A 15-year-old was in group therapy on an inpatient unit. He complained that he did not like the staff running the unit and that he had many important things he could talk about but would not do so because of this dislike. A little later he returned to the subject and said that he knew the therapist running the group probably wanted to know the things he could have talked about. The therapist feigned ignorance, asking the patient what he was referring to and adding that he had found it hard to listen to the patient earlier and had tuned him out. The patient protested that this was disrespectful, and the therapist admitted it, adding, "But you're really boring, and it's hard to listen to you. Sorry." The patient spent the remainder of the group session in evident distress, furious with the therapist.

One 16-year-old drug-dealing youth was extremely bright and used his intelligence to outwit those trying to help him. He came to treatment well prepared to out-talk his new therapist. After several sessions in which the therapist listened appreciatively as the patient told how he defeated previous treatment efforts, the therapist suddenly fell silent except for occasionally asking, "What exactly did you want to work on?" The patient then started to talk about subjects that were in fact important, but he talked about them in a patently false manner; it was clear he was acting the part of an earnest patient but meant nothing he said. The therapist then began to look sleepy and kept nodding off. Eventually he seemed to fall completely asleep. The patient fell silent and appeared a little confused. The therapist startled awake and asked if he had missed anything important. The patient was offended but did not want to show it. This interaction was repeated several times until the patient began to speak of how insignificant he felt when the therapist nodded off, signaling a change in the direction of the case.

A 16-year-old girl told the therapist she had nothing to work on, that she was in treatment simply because she was made to be. After two sessions in which the therapist learned more history but could find no way to connect with the patient, he decided to fall silent. At first the patient grew silent too, but after twenty minutes protested. The therapist said he thought it was the patient's responsibility to bring something to talk about, not his, and he fell quiet again. The patient tried hard to feign indifference, but the silence bothered her. After forty minutes she could not take it any longer and suddenly bolted from the office. The therapist was caught off guard and so was not able to stop her, but the session nonetheless proved to be a turning point in getting the girl engaged.

A late-adolescent patient was exerting a powerful influence over his peers at a residential center. He had a way of appearing superior to his peers, and they tended to pursue him, hoping he would like them. The staff decided they needed to reduce his status with his peers. In group therapy they would call on him to talk about some issue, only to cut him off after a few minutes by saying, "I'm not interested in that. Talk about something else." Whether the patient responded with a protest or with a new topic, the staff would then appear impatient, saying, "This is not my idea of therapy! You've got to learn to do better than this!" They would then call on someone else, dismissing the patient. This effectively ended the patient's ability to appear superior to his peers, who then started to press him to improve.

In all of these interventions, the therapist is trying, in essence, *to be more narcissistic than the patient.* This is precisely the response that makes it difficult for the patient to continue his or her own narcissistic presentation. The narcissistic patient is prepared to be indifferent or scornful toward others or to receive their adulation; the therapist, however, interferes with what the patient is prepared for by assuming a narcissistic posture with the patient. This is the stance that interferes with the type of interaction narcissistic patients prefer and forces them to adopt a style of interaction out of their comfort zone. By doing this, therapists become a problem for narcissistic patients, a problem that can only be solved as the patients find a different way to experience self and other, one not built on narcissism.

Controlling the Patient's Reaction

Narcissistic adolescents are not likely to enjoy or appreciate the therapist's attempts to adopt a narcissistic stance and, from that stance, to deflate them. Their reaction will almost certainly be one of anger,

although a significant minority may become more subdued and confused than angry. In their anger, patients may try to leave sessions,
attack the therapist verbally and perhaps physically, persuade their
parents to take them out of treatment, or find another way to react
that will return them to a narcissistic stance. The therapist must be
prepared for each of these responses.

When working with narcissistic adolescents on an outpatient basis,
some care must be taken with patients who might react aggressively
within the session. The most likely form of aggression will be an
attempt to leave the office. Therapists can decrease this eventuality
by sitting between the patient and the door. In addition, therapists
may ask for parental help, arranging for the parents to sit just outside
the door in order to help if the need arises. When therapists feel they
are not in a position to prevent the patient's leaving the office, they
may have to content themselves with predicting the patient's flight
before it occurs, saying, for instance, "I doubt you have the experience to handle this situation. Any minute now you'll have to get up
and leave." In such a case, parents should be coached to tell the patient
that the therapist had told them the patient would probably have to
run from a session soon.

There is always the risk that a narcissistic patient will become
assaultive with the therapist. In my judgment there is no way to treat
narcissistic adolescents without taking this risk. If therapists find themselves too afraid of a patient to inflict the narcissistic wound that is
needed, they probably should stop the treatment. If the therapist
cannot become more narcissistic than the patient, the resistance is
not likely to end, and a frightened therapist is not likely to be a successful narcissist.

Assuming the patient is not assaultive and can be kept in the therapist's office, the chief problem is responding to the patient's protests.
The therapist must find ways to define the patient's reaction to the
therapist as inadequate. The therapist may compare the patient's reaction unfavorably with that of other patients or may criticize the
patient's response on other grounds. The key is that the therapist does
not relinquish the role of judge or critic to the patient but maintains
this role.

In an outpatient group therapy, a therapist had been trying to deflate one of the narcissistic patients, who was responding by attacking the therapist verbally, saying that she had been making progress but now felt that there was no point in trying further, that the therapist had robbed her of all desire to work on her problems. "I may as well give up completely," she said in an obvious attempt to win support from her peers who, she hoped, would take her side. The therapist began telling the group that his own daughter used to have such reactions whenever she had tried to do something hard and was unable to reach her goal. She would, he said, eventually grow angry and make a mess of the whole enterprise, destroying everything she had done rather than endure the frustration. He paused and for a moment seemed a little sympathetic to the patient until he added that this usually occurred when his daughter was 2 or so, playing with blocks, a comment that led other group members to laugh at the angry patient, thereby aggravating the narcissistic wound.

A 13-year-old patient told the therapist that he was not helping her, that he was just making her upset and needed to be more encouraging. The therapist replied that it was arrogant and contemptuous for the patient to believe she knew as much as he did about how the session should be run. He deliberately used these words, assuming correctly that the patient would have to ask what they meant, thereby reinforcing the picture of the patient as inadequate.

The therapist must be comfortable with the patient's anger or dismay and be prepared to sustain the tension level in the room until the patient begins to move away from a narcissistic stance. On the other hand, this is not something the therapist should enjoy very much. I have already noted that this style of interaction is inherently aggressive in nature, drawing on the sadism that is unhappily available to us all. If therapists find themselves becoming excited or "hyped" by the types of interactions described in this chapter, they should not use them or at the very least should obtain consultation on those cases. The danger is that the excitement the therapist feels is a sign of inflation, a sign that the therapist has moved into a narcissistic universe and is no longer intervening with the patient's best interests at heart. A grandiose, inflated therapist may inflict narcissistic injuries for the excitement that comes from doing so, an excitement that flows from fantasies of being the omnipotent baby in the arms of the adoring mother of fusion. It is important that the therapist not give in to such regressive, albeit attractive, fantasies. What the therapist does must be done deliberately, without undue excitement and willingly given up when it is time to move to a different style of interaction.

Moving the Patient away from a Narcissistic Style

At some point the therapist must discontinue the assault on the patient's grandiosity, and there are no hard-and-fast rules on when this change should be made. Indefinitely continuing to injure the patient's narcissism inevitably becomes sadistic, and the best that can be hoped for is a battle of wills to see whether the patient or therapist will be the first to give in. Infinitely more preferable is for the therapist to stay in a position to offer a more mature and helpful pattern of interaction when the patient is willing. It is sometimes necessary to refer the patient to a new therapist. The patient may be too angry to submit to the person who made such an assault on his or her grandiosity but might be willing to start over with someone new. Before giving up, though, efforts should be made to move the patient away from a narcissistic style.

The first step in accomplishing this is to confirm that the patient has good reason to be angry with the therapist. This confirmation must not be done apologetically but matter of factly. The therapist should simply acknowledge that the patient is angry and that the therapist realizes there is good reason for this, that he or she has in fact behaved in ways that would make most persons angry. The therapist is showing a willingness to frustrate the patient and at the same time offer the satisfaction of accepting the patient's complaints about the frustration.

The therapist should not try to explain away the patient's anger or do anything to water down the fact that the therapist *caused* the anger. There is no good reason to define the anger as a transference reaction or to suggest, for instance, that the patient gets angry in related situations and should work on this problem. In a straightforward manner, the therapist must admit that the patient has reason to be angry, that most persons are angry when they are told things that are hard to hear or even insulting. Without apologizing or in any way taking back what was said, the therapist must accept responsibility for the offense given to the patient, acknowledge the distress this caused, and sympathize with the patient's upset.

Therapists must maintain their willingness to wound the patient and accept responsibility for the consequent upset until they begin to sense chances to become more affiliative. At times it will be obvious when a patient is ready to "give in." Patients may signal such readiness by openly admitting that the therapist was correct on some point that had earlier been disputed, or they may ask for help with a problem, presenting the issue in a way that seems more genuine than before.

> One patient started a session by saying that she had been "arrogant and inappropriate" in earlier sessions. The therapist recognized this as a sign the patient was ready to move to a new type of interaction. He asked the patient how she had come to believe this and what he could do to help her master the problem. This exchange essentially ended the period of open resistance and began a period when the patient was willing to make some effort, even though she was not as fully allied with treatment as the therapist would have preferred.

Most patients do not openly state a willingness to end resistance. Therapists may simply sense a lessening of the tension in sessions or sense some increase in the patient's openness. Parents may report improvement or state that the patient is quoting the therapist in ways that seem positive. In other cases there may be no evidence the patient is willing to change the style of interaction with the therapist; the therapist must simply try a more affiliative approach and watch the patient's reaction.

> The patient whose therapist had said he was silent because the patient had said nothing worth responding to became angry and anxious in sessions. He was clearly offended at what the therapist had said and uneasy at the prospect of more insults. He did not

really produce new and significant material in subsequent sessions, but he did appear to be trying to figure out what the therapist would endorse. Since this implied a move away from a narcissistic stance, the therapist praised the patient for his perseverance. This compliment was deliberately chosen; the patient had tended to give up easily when thwarted in school and in relationships. The patient was relieved at this (deserved) compliment, and treatment moved to a more conventional phase.

If the therapist has inflicted a narcissistic wound and afterwards maintained the stance of someone who continues to evaluate and judge the patient, then any willingness by the patient to be more affiliative has the character of submission. This is precisely what the therapist seeks: submission to a benevolent authority is the movement that begins to end infantile megalomania in early childhood and is what the therapist wants from the narcissistic adolescent in treatment. With such a development, the resistance phase of treatment is effectively ended, and the therapist is in a better position to use conventional treatment approaches. The only exception occurs when the patient moves away from narcissistic resistance to another type of resistance; in such a case the therapist will have to adjust his or her response accordingly (cf. Eissler 1958).

CONCLUSION

The therapist has ended the patient's narcissistic resistance by assuming a stance inconsistent with the patient's narcissism. It was Leary's (1957) conclusion that human behavior is not private and insulated but interpersonal. If this is true, then how any of us behaves will depend to a great degree on the response others give. It is difficult to continue a certain style of behavior if the response others make is thoroughly incongruous or inconsistent with the response we intended to pull from them. The therapist has tried to behave in a way that is inconsistent with the patient's grandiosity. In essence this means that the therapist has had to become more narcissistic than the patient.

CHAPTER 5

MASOCHISTIC RESISTANCE

PRESENTING PICTURE

It has already been noted that there is no one-to-one correspondence between the out-of-control patient's presenting symptoms and the style of resistance he or she will use in therapy. No matter what type of resistance is used, the patient is likely to show a combination of behavior problems, drug use, and symptoms that suggest some affective syndrome. In general this holds for patients who show masochistic resistance as well: on the basis of presenting complaints alone, a therapist will probably not be able to predict that a patient will show a masochistic style.

Masochistic adolescents do, however, seem more obviously depressed than adolescents showing other types of resistance, and this may be a clue to the therapist. In addition, anecdotal evidence suggests two other aids in coming to an early diagnosis of masochistic resistance. First, in spite of their depression, masochistic patients are not likely to have tried to harm themselves. Suicide attempts and self-mutilation are not typical. Second, although they are less likely to have harmed themselves, they are more likely to have been harmed by others. These are the patients most likely to be physically beaten up and/or to have been taken advantage of sexually. Consequently, therapists may be alerted to the possibility of masochistic resistance when the patient is obviously depressed, shows no history of self-harm, and has a history of having been hurt by others.

THE APPEARANCE OF WANTING HELP

Patients who show masochistic resistance are not likely to appear masochistic in their first encounters with the therapist. Initially they will appear depressed, in pain, and therefore willing to accept help. The truth of the matter turns out to be rather different. After a time it will become clear to the therapist that these patients are more intent on showing they can't be helped than on making use of treatment. At first, though, the masochistic adolescent may appear to be someone who can and wants to benefit from therapy.

This initial good impression stems from certain traits associated with a masochistic style. In their first encounters with the therapist these patients are usually submissive, seemingly dependent individuals. They appear to be looking for someone who can tell them what to do, and they often appear grateful for the therapist's attentiveness and suggestions. There is frequently a kind of shy weakness about them that can be appealing, at least at first. These traits make it easy for the therapist to feel strong, wise, and needed. While experienced therapists may have an easier time resisting these (countertransferential) reactions than novices, the patient is likely to be accomplished at making others want to reach out in a helpful way.

There is something about persons who are in pain that pulls warm interest and concern from most people, and masochistic adolescents do appear to be in pain—as noted, they appear depressed. In addition many adults harbor a quiet desire to be important to an adolescent; there is a narcissistic satisfaction in feeling important to someone who, because of age, does not accord most adults the status of being important. The adolescent who shows masochistic resistance has these advantages, then, and can briefly appear to be a promising patient.

Kaiser (1965) suggested that every patient shows what he termed the "universal symptom," or duplicity, and that it is therefore important to uncover the way that the patient is not entirely what he or she seems to be but is dissembling in some manner. On this theory, therapists should assume that every patient, no matter what the presentation in the session, is being dishonest in some important and revealing way. This is not to say that every patient consciously lies to or deceives the therapist, although this certainly happens. It is to say that "what you see is not what you get" most of the time in therapy.

This is nowhere more true than with masochistic adolescents. While first encounters may lead the therapist to believe that the patient is someone who wants help, this is the wrong conclusion. In fact the masochistic adolescent is someone who wants to persuade others to try to help—and even to become invested in helping—but who has no intention of accepting the help that is offered. While the patient may appear to be a dependent and potentially pliable individual, the patient's actual intent is to broadcast inferiority and utter weakness.

A parallel interaction may take place between masochistic adolescents and their peers. At first these youth may be accepted by their peers, who respond to many of the same traits that appeal to the therapist: the patient's docility, seeming agreeableness, and the appearance of needing others. Sooner or later, however, the masochistic youth will be rejected, taken advantage of, or physically or sexually abused. They seem to call out the other person's sadism, in sharp contrast to the favorable impression they may make at first.

A 16-year-old girl was admitted to a residential center. At first her peers saw her as somewhat shy and winsome. She was described as "sweet" by several and seemed to be someone who was having a hard time and needed help. After two weeks, however, nearly all of her peers were furious with her. In almost every unit activity, her peers managed to attack her for something, always reducing her to tears. The self-deprecating and apologetic responses she made at these times, oddly enough, seemed to aggravate everyone even further. She had moved from being accepted to being the unit's scapegoat by being relentlessly weak and inept, eventually eliciting scorn and contempt from her peers.

It seems important to masochistic patients to disappoint the other, in this case the therapist, but in an odd way. The masochistic patient seems drawn to interactions that would make most persons uneasy in the extreme, interactions in which the other is encouraged in a grandiose direction, then deflated. Encouraged to feel immensely helpful to the patient, the therapist's ultimate ineffectuality is revealed. The result is that the therapist feels first deflated, then angry and contemptuous toward the person who effected the deflation, the patient.

What is so interesting about this interaction is that it is essentially sadistic, not masochistic. In fact, a sadistic individual might well use this very ploy, first inducing the therapist to feel helpful and then letting the therapist in on the secret that the supposed help had not been helpful at all. The therapist, in the hands of the sadistic patient, is then left feeling deflated and useless. This is the very interaction that takes place with the masochistic patient as well except that the therapist's feelings do not stop with deflation and uselessness but quickly move to irritation and anger at the patient. The patient manages to induce in the therapist the very feelings that then get turned on the patient.

The same thing happens with other people in the patient's life, although there are other triggers. The trigger for the therapist is the patient's having accepted and valued the therapist's help, only to devalue it later. With peers the patient may behave in an angry, demanding, or docile, needy fashion until the other person becomes angry and lashes out or ends the relationship. The patient may be utterly out of touch with what is going on with those nearby, managing to provoke them into some sort of attack, perhaps even a physical or sexual attack, through his or her seeming obliviousness. In all these cases the patient is behaving in ways that are colored with sadism, either through a greedy aggressiveness that eventually brings attack or rebuff from the other person or through a determined effort to make caretakers feel helpless and ineffectual. The only thing that separates the masochist from the sadist is that the former manages to make the sadism come back in his or her direction.

Matters do not, then, turn out as they begin with masochistic adolescents. The therapist may at first feel pleased with the case, believing the patient's evident distress is a sign there will be motivation to work hard and feeling too that the patient is someone who may even appreciate the therapist's efforts. Despite these bright promises, the case early takes a nasty turn, leaving a therapist who was optimistic feeling "had."

There are two basic types of masochistic resistance, the first of which may be called *angry* masochism, and the second of which may be termed *docile* masochism. Each will be discussed in turn.

ANGRY MASOCHISM

Angry masochistic patients are those whose demandingness is what eventually turns others against them. They present themselves as weak and helpless but then tend to make their helplessness into the other person's problem. They can be counted on not to cooperate with the other's attempts to help, and at the same time they manage to leave the impression that the other has somehow failed them by not helping. Eventually the other person becomes angry and even abusive.

The patient's experience of these interactions is different from the other person's experience. The patient typically feels ashamed of needing anything from the other person and is angry both with the self for being in need and at the other person for being needed. The shame and anger do not stop the patient from making demands on the other; there is a near compulsion in fact to look to the other for assistance or to impose in some fashion. However, the patient clearly finds it distasteful to be in need and so asks for and accepts the help in a manner that makes it utterly unpleasant for both parties. The patient shows gratitude only briefly and then adds resentment or makes more demands.

This combination of demandingness and lack of any genuine appreciation makes the other feel that the patient is incapable of giving something back. The relationship is therefore one-sided, and the other person begins to experience the patient as a burden or drain. Whatever good will may have existed initially begins to fade and to be replaced with aggravation and resentment. In any healthy relationship, there must be some sense of mutuality, the sense that each person can know and appreciate the other and can at least contribute that knowledge and appreciation to the relationship. The angry masochist is not able to leave a fairly narrow, self-absorbed world in which the other person is used but neither known nor valued as an independent person.

The angry masochist cannot really accept the help that is offered. This is not because the other person is experienced as having offered insufficient or inadequate help or as having taken advantage in the process of helping, as would be the case with paranoid patients. Rather, the help is not accepted because the patient feels it would somehow compromise his or her independence or integrity. Of course, this is quite dishonest: The patient is not behaving independently and is in fact embroiled in dependency on the other. The patient is trying nonetheless to avoid feeling needy on the one hand while behaving in an aggressively needy fashion on the other. The effect is to make the patient's neediness a problem for the other but not for the patient. The other person may then feel very much as if the masochistic patient were reacting in a paranoid fashion; the other may feel accused of having done something wrong when all that was intended was to offer help. At the very least, the other person will feel put upon and taken advantage of.

In sessions patients who show angry masochistic resistance tend to be pushy and demanding, all the while letting the therapist know that they cannot possibly do for themselves what the therapist is supposed to do. They manage to make demands, become angry when their demands are not immediately met, and parade their own ineptitude and helplessness—all at the same time. There is a kind of entitlement to their helplessness, as though they have a bargain with the therapist: if I am helpless, you have to do things for me. The entitlement is hidden behind tearfulness and irritable depression, and so it is hard to see, often leaving the therapist aggravated without quite knowing why. Attempts to set limits on the patient's demandingness are likely to be met with displays of just how helpless the patient can be.

One adolescent girl asked her therapist for many notes, letters, and phone calls to her school. She wanted the therapist to take her side against unfair teachers who did not appreciate "what I'm going through." At first it seemed as if some discussion with school personnel was in order; the patient seemed depressed and unable to keep up with her work, and the therapist thought it might make sense for teachers to be aware of this situation. However, the patient felt victimized in many ways by teachers and school administrators and very often wanted the therapist to offer an excuse for why she should not have to meet expectations. When the therapist indicated he thought the patient should be the one to discuss problems with teachers and the school's principal, she grew withdrawn and barely able to speak in the session. The therapist felt he was being punished and controlled by the patient's helplessness.

A freshman in college sought services at the university's clinic. He was depressed, he said, and already far behind in his studies. He also felt alone, as though he could not make friends among the people in his dormitory or in his classes. The therapist immediately felt an interest in the patient, identifying perhaps with some of his complaints. Yet when the therapist sought more information, the patient suddenly announced that he did not know if he could talk about it any further and turned his chair toward the wall, with his back to the therapist. There the patient sat for the remainder of the session, sometimes seeming to cry and never able to articulate his problems beyond his initial description.

It is impossible to predict with precision how a patient will react when his or her initial resistance ends. As noted earlier, some patients will move to the heart of their problems and settle down to a more typical therapeutic process. Others will move to a different type of resistance. My impression is that patients who begin with angry masochistic resistance tend to move toward a paranoid style of resistance as their initial resistance is undermined by the therapist.

DOCILE MASOCHISM

Patients showing a docile, masochistic style are the most resistant to treatment of all out-of-control adolescents. Their very docility makes it difficult to induce change; whatever pressure the therapist places on them is simply absorbed. What seems most to be missing is shame. While the angry masochist is ashamed at being in need, the docile masochist feels no lasting unease at his or her weakness (even though the patient may make a protest to the contrary). There is therefore no strong motivation to give it up. The friend, teacher, or therapist encounters passivity and weakness and little else.

From the standpoint of the other person, the docile masochistic patient should be ashamed, which is to say that the other person would be ashamed to be so weak. These patients are the types of people who make others cringe at their helplessness—they manage to make others feel embarrassed for them, inducing a kind of temporary identification in which the observer is suddenly aware of what he or she would feel in the patient's place: shame at being so inept or at looking silly. The result is either a desire to get away altogether or a desire to degrade the patient.

In either case the other person's response is built on scorn and contempt. The angry masochist draws resentful anger, while the docile masochist draws scorn. Most individuals are fairly polite about how they show scorn; most will simply want to avoid the masochistic patient, their active disinterest broken only by a slight feeling of disgust. Indifference, however, is merely a civilized version of contempt, and the masochistic patient can often draw much less civilized versions. Individuals who are at all sadistically inclined will be drawn to abuse and take advantage of the docile masochist. Hence, a number of patients will present themselves with dating histories that involve physical abuse and repeated rapes.

> One narcissistic adolescent described his dating relationship with an obviously masochistic girl. He said that the two had sex frequently and that what "really turned me on" was the girl's embarrassment and discomfort during sex. The more the girl did not want to have sex, the more the boy did, until he would almost force himself on

her. This pattern of coercive intercourse would often occur several times daily. The boy seemed particularly to enjoy the times when the girl cried. It turned out that she did little else to dissuade him and willingly went out with him time after time. He took advantage of her in other ways too, dating other girls and flaunting this. However, the girl put up with whatever the boy wanted to do, her docility and distress evoking sadism from him.

A 13-year-old boy was placed in boarding school by his mother, who was herself quite masochistic and with whom her son was physically aggressive. In the school, his peers quickly started to pick on him, regularly beating him up. These physical attacks occurred irrespective of his behavior; whether he tried to please them or not, his peers would attack him. He could not make himself put up a defense. Each attack served to make him more obsequious and passive. By the time he left the school, he was being beaten almost nightly.

The docile masochist draws contempt through being open to it. There is often a quiet communication from the masochistic adolescent that invites the other to be degrading. This communication is made through body language, through the way the patient stands, holds his or her head, makes or fails to make eye contact, and through the tone of voice. The overall effect of these communications is unmistakable—to invite others to do whatever they wish, communicating that no effort will be made to preserve pride or place.

In case the communication is missed, the patient's manner of interacting with others reiterates it. Docile masochistic patients have a way of being subtly aggravating. They seem so helpless, so much in need of assistance. Those who are sadistically inclined will feel this helplessness as an invitation to take advantage. Others who are not especially sadistic may find it automatic to reach out to these patients in helpful ways only to find that their attempts to be helpful never quite turn out as they intended. They may find that the patient did not accept their help for some reason or responded to it in a way guaranteed to botch the task. The would-be helper eventually feels used up and drained, and also aggravated that the patient is just as much in need at the end of the day as at the start. The consequence is scorn for the patient who just a little earlier was seen more fondly, as someone in need of help.

Therapists may find their own feelings to be an aid in diagnosis. Just as the angry masochist can evoke resentment and anger from would-be helpers, the docile masochist evokes sadism or a lust to dominate and hurt the weaker party. Many persons, including therapists, are not especially comfortable with such feelings and tend not to be aware of them, only to express those feelings later in behavior. It is an aid for therapists to remain open to the feelings patients evoke; in this case it is an aid to find that the patient seems to evoke anger and/or contempt (expressed as sadism). This may mean that the patient is showing masochistic resistance.

THE AVOIDANCE OF INITIATIVE

Whether the patient shows an angry or docile masochistic style, or some combination of the two, the result is that the other person is completely in charge. This appears to be the overarching goal of a masochistic style, to surrender one's own will in favor of the other's wishes (Menaker 1979, Reich 1940/1973). The docility and helplessness shown by these patients is certainly designed to broadcast their inferiority, but these traits also imply a certain image of the other person, that the other is powerful and superior. These patients flood the other with narcissistic deference and submission, sometimes gladly and sometimes resentfully, but in either case with the clear message that the other is due all that the patient is not. The rough treatment these patients eventually receive comes from the fact that human beings are generally at their very worst when operating in the pure ether of narcissism. Inevitably, the worst truths about us are realized in that atmosphere; the patient's demands and weaknesses finally communicate that the other is supposed to be utterly in charge, which awakens the unflattering behavior human beings always show when thinking of themselves as gods.

Thus, the masochistic style invites the other's narcissism. And yet earlier I suggested that the masochistic style itself contains considerable sadism, that the masochist's behavior might very well be shown by a sadistic individual—the only difference being that the sadist would keep the sadism turned against the other person rather than let it come back on the self. How can masochism imply worshipful submission on the one hand and be built on sadism on the other hand?

We should start an answer to this question with Annie Reich's (1940/1973) observations about one of her adult patients who manifested complete incapacity to do anything on her own. This patient could make herself act only if the other took the initiative; she would follow the other's instructions blindly and agree with anyone in conversation. She seemed to be jettisoning the experience of initiative, avoiding any behavior that might imply separateness or autonomous strivings. As she lowered her expectations of herself, she inflated her vision of the other, often idealizing the men in her life, for instance. Reich speculated that such patients seek to preserve the illusion of fusion with the mother. Union with others who are seen as great and mighty can equal magical oneness with the mother. Consequently, the surrender of initiative to an idealized other may express the desire to be a very young child in the arms of an omnipotent mother.

Menaker (1979) also saw masochistic traits as defenses against separation from the mother, or from her successors. She pointed out that masochistic submission is a normal part of growing up, as the young child must surrender his or her own wishes to the rules and restrictions of the parents and the larger world. In this generally benevolent submission, the child is not harmed, since the submission takes place in the context of love and belonging. If, however, the child's naturally unfolding demands for self-assertion and autonomy are met with anger or rejection by the parents, the child may learn that independence in any form equals loss of love, while the surrender of autonomous strivings equals connectedness. In such a sequence, masochism is the patient's defense against loss of love.

Masochism, therefore, is not a maneuver designed to elicit sadism from the other but a maneuver aimed at submitting to the other. It is a style based on surrender, an effort at ridding the self of autonomy and evoking domination. The masochist does not seek pain—which the early psychoanalytic writers supposed as they operated from an instinct model of personality, in which masochism was essentially a libidinal urge that carried the satisfaction gained from the expression of any libidinal striving. Rather, it is an attempt to adapt to a world in which autonomy threatened the young child with abandonment. In psychoanalytic terms, it is an ego function, a defense against behavior that would threaten the child's survival (Berliner 1940).

The masochistic patient is not trying to evoke sadism from the other person but a domination associated with caretaking. When the patient is provocative (the angry masochist) he or she is trying to make others prove their superiority, their ability to make the decisions and tell the patient how things should proceed. To the extent the patient is utterly submissive (the docile masochist), this docility and lack of will are declarations that the other is indeed expected to be dominant and that the patient will show no resistance to the ongoing superiority—the patient only shows resistance to the possibility of becoming competent or capable.

In treatment, therapists tend to try to move their patients toward success and independence. This may be particularly high on the therapist's unspoken agenda when working with adolescents, since therapists will assume that adolescent patients are keen on getting away from adult control and building their own separate lives, or at least the capacity for such separateness. However, such tendencies and assumptions fly in the face of the masochistic agenda and reawaken old issues of whether the child's autonomous strivings are acceptable.

Therapists may think they are trying to help patients solve problems and become more capable of standing on their own. This is not, unhappily, how the matter will look to these patients. The masochistic adolescent is not trying to be helped but to be dominated. For this reason, the patient will react to therapists' plans, ideas, suggestions, encouragement, and interpretations almost as if they were traps designed to fool the patient into showing the autonomous strivings that had so long been hidden and suppressed. Masochistic patients must then reassure their therapists that they have no independent urges and intend to remain helpless. In addition they must interact with their therapists in ways that coerce the therapist to remain powerful and omnipotent: they are helpless in order to make the therapist dominate them.

It is undeniable, though, that there is some sadism in the patient's interactions with the therapist. After all, the therapist is being invited to dominate the situation but *only on the patient's terms*. There is a paradox in the masochistic patient's interactions with the therapist. On the one hand, the therapist is invited (or forced) to set the agenda, but if the agenda is for the patient to become stronger the patient in effect shows resistance. How is it that a patient who is committed to being dominated manages to resist in this (or any other) fashion? Considering how helpless these patients seem, they have a surprising knack for making the therapist feel stymied.

Anyone who has tried to work with these patients, who seem allergic to any show of willfulness, knows that they are in fact quite stubborn. They have managed to suborn their autonomous strivings into a commitment to inferiority, in effect, and they cling to this inferiority *independent* of any effort the therapist may make. In other words, their helplessness is itself an expression of autonomy, a protest against the demand that independence be surrendered completely. They then cling to helplessness fiercely and with determination, feeling that the therapist's urgings to become more potent are in actuality a demand to surrender this last bastion of independence.

The masochistic patient's sadism, therefore, is genuine. Sadism is a matter of power, and the masochistic patient clings to a single powerful element, the ability to defeat anyone who might wish to move the patient away from being dominated. Therapy is therefore a power struggle, with the patient clinging to powerlessness and determined willfully to defeat the therapist's attempt to move the patient toward any stance that might imply initiative. Once therapists realize this, they have the tools needed to defeat the patient in this struggle.

THERAPY AS A STRUGGLE FOR POWERLESSNESS

The therapist's task with the masochistic adolescent is, first, to refuse to dominate the patient and, second, to move the patient toward a stance that is incompatible with powerlessness. The therapist's chief weapon in this struggle is the realization that masochistic patients require the therapist to assume a role complementary to their power-lessness and lack of initiative. A further aid is the fact that the ado-lescent personality is not yet established, that independence and autonomy are still existential possibilities for these patients. In a sense, in fact, the adolescent masochist is striving for independence, but the only type of independence allowed in the masochistic scheme of things is the willful resistance of independence (and its implied threat of separateness).

Therapists must therefore assume a stance that is incompatible with the role the masochistic adolescent needs the therapist to play. If the patient needs the therapist to be dominating and powerful, then the therapist must be the reverse of these things. By behaving in a way incompatible with what the patient wants, the therapist makes the patient's own behavior untenable. As with most patterns of experi-ence and behavior, masochism places demands on the other to play a certain role, and if the other fails to play the required part, the masochist will have trouble maintaining his or her experience of the self as helpless and inferior.

Therapists must adopt what is essentially a masochistic stance, perhaps becoming more masochistic than the patient. They may do this by telling the patient that they are baffled about what to do or say in this case, that they feel badly about this failure, and that they truly do not know how to help the patient. While therapists should not go so far as to display depressive affect for the patient, they should parade doubt, indecision, confusion, and futility about the case. By behaving in these ways, therapists will refuse the role the patient prefers that they play, the part of someone whose dominance relieves the patient of all initiative.

A late adolescent with a very long history of heavy alcohol and drug use came to treatment with complaints of depression. The patient did in fact appear to be severely depressed, but he also seemed surprisingly comfortable to feel that way. Many previous outpatient treatments and two inpatient stays had not arrested his progres-sive deterioration throughout adolescence. While the patient was willing to take antidepressant medication, he was unwilling to do anything else that might change his situation. He did not respond when the therapist tried to explore the dynamics of the patient's situation and expressed confusion at the therapist's questions. The therapist changed his approach and began to press the patient to leave his house occasionally to be with other people, to resume his former participation in Alcoholics Anonymous, and, finally, to find a part-time job as a way to structure the patient's excessive free time. The patient then fairly quickly began to regress and used threats of suicide to force his family to hospitalize him.

In a session during the second week in the hospital, the therapist changed his approach yet again and began to express an attitude of helplessness to the patient. He described all that he had tried and said he thought he had made the patient worse. He apologized to the patient, said he was confused by the case, reported that he had sought consultation to get new ideas but found the consultant baffled also, and then added several times, "I have no idea how to help you, and I feel terrible about it." During the session the patient seemed unmoved by the therapist's remarks and said little beyond how depressed he felt. However, the patient's family called the next day to say that the patient had been agitated by the therapist's remarks and had talked nervously about this throughout their visit later in the day. The next day the patient began for the first time to show an interest in earning a higher level on the unit. The family reported one day later that the patient had finally taken an active part in family therapy and added that the patient had even talked about getting a job when he was discharged.

The rationale for this approach is simple. The patient seeks to place the therapist in a position of superiority, avoiding any behavior that might express initiative or imply separateness. The therapist refuses this stance, instead showing passivity and lack of strength. In essence this is a refusal of the power struggle the patient seeks to create; the therapist refuses the invitation to try to make the patient competent, focusing instead entirely on his or her own ineffectuality and grinding to a passive halt.

The patient is left without the usual indirect way to express independence. The patient's only grasp on independence was his or her stubborn resistance of any effort to elicit successful, competent behavior. The therapist not only refuses to try to elicit such behavior but actually places the patient in a position of having to try to evoke such behavior from the therapist. The tables are turned, in effect—if the patient is to maintain (the preferred indirect hold on) autonomy, it can no longer be through defying the therapist's efforts to elicit competence and must instead be through trying to elicit competence from the therapist. The therapist, however, should not cooperate with this effort. Until the patient is willing to abandon masochistic resistance, the therapist must remain helpless and apparently baffled by the case.

The patient's first reaction will usually be to try to force the therapist out of the masochistic role, usually through becoming more masochistic, which is to say more wretched, passive, and depressed. When the patient escalates in this way, the therapist must escalate too, becoming even more confused and puzzled, expressing more dismay and offering new apologies in the face of the patient's seeming distress. If the therapist does this, the interaction is at an impasse, and the patient has to make a choice—whether to continue being helpless, even though the therapist refuses the complementary role, or seek a different type of interaction.

At this point the therapist hopes to see some sign of anger from the patient. Anger would be evidence that the patient is giving up passivity and is beginning to push against the therapist. Anger would therefore imply opposition to the therapist, which in turn implies some growing measure of independence. Anger involves making a protest of some sort, and protest is not passive. It implies a capacity for criticism of the other or for making critical judgments. Therefore, a masochistic patient who becomes angry is in an untenable position, since anger leads away from submission and the refusal of initiative.

In group therapy a middle adolescent female began reciting the many, many ways her mother had abused and taken advantage of her. This was a very frequent event in the life of the group. Initially her peers had been sympathetic and had offered support. However, they grew bored with the patient's recitations, which never really changed. At first the other patients suggested ways to make progress on the relationship with the mother, but when these suggestions were either discounted or ignored, they became impatient and irritated. Finally, the other patients either ignored this girl altogether or attacked her when she spoke. One day the patient started to tell the group yet again of the many times her mother had ignored her, cursed at her, or deprived her of something she needed, which led to the following exchange.

THERAPIST: I feel bad about what you're saying because it is clear we haven't been much help to you with this problem, and I just don't know how to help with this. I feel terrible we haven't helped you any.

PATIENT: [is surprised but says nothing and hangs her head]

THERAPIST: I just don't think we can do anything with this.

PATIENT: [remains silent but seems angry]

THERAPIST: We're in a position where I don't think there's a lot we can do.

PATIENT: [remains mute and keeps looking at the floor]

THERAPIST: That's why I said I was confused. What do you expect from us?

PATIENT: [angrily] I don't know what I'm expecting! It'd be easier if someone told me what to feel!

THERAPIST: Well, I think we're stuck.

In this exchange, the therapist has surprised the patient with his approach. She has responded provocatively by her withdrawal, inviting the therapist to step into the void she leaves by her silence and again take control or dominate her. She wants him to return to the role of someone who is all-knowing and wise. When he refuses she remains utterly passive, leaving a vacuum in the group. The therapist should probably have let her remain silent for ten or fifteen minutes before again professing helplessness and moving to a new patient. Instead he asks the patient what she expects, and her reply is classically masochistic: she professes her own helplessness ("I don't know what I'm expecting") and asks to be defined ("it'd be easier if someone told me what to feel"). The therapist then returns to a masochistic response ("we're stuck") and moves on to another patient.

In this case the therapist's masochistic approach should be continued. The patient was angry at the therapist, and it would not have been difficult to get this out in the open. Once a masochistic patient openly shows anger at the therapist, the interaction is changed, and the patient has become much more accessible.

Later in the same group therapy session, a late adolescent male presented a masochistic style the therapists felt was fake, designed to elicit sympathy from his peers. Even though the patient had for a long time been aggressive and belligerent with his parents and other authority figures, he claimed in this session that he felt terribly guilty about such behavior. The therapists were certain this was not true and felt the patient was trying to avoid any genuine revelation about himself and his motives. In order to bring about something more genuine from the patient, one of the therapists adopted a masochistic style.

THERAPIST: You've talked about your parents before, and I feel we haven't been much help to you. Now here you are feeling bad, it looks like, and I feel like we've just wasted your time. You know, we haven't helped you at all.

PATIENT: You've not wasted my time.

THERAPIST: Oh, I know we have, and I feel just like we should have been some help by now. I feel bad about not helping you.

PATIENT: Don't feel that. It's not your fault.

THERAPIST: But here you are now feeling guilty, and that's painful. We should have been able to help you feel better.

PATIENT: Lots of time I feel guilty. It's not your fault.

THERAPIST: Well, I just wish we could have helped you.

PATIENT: [clearly irritated] I'm confused. You have helped me.

THERAPIST: It sounds like you don't trust my judgment about this.

PATIENT: I do trust you, at least in this group. The other group I was in didn't understand me, and I wouldn't tell them shit. They would just throw issues up in your face, and you couldn't say nothin' to them. [The therapist] never stopped it, so I didn't ever say anything.

The therapist believes that the patient is actually angry and defiant and seeks to disguise this orientation under a false masochism.

The therapist therefore adopts a masochistic style with the patient, who initially clings to his own masochism. However, he becomes angry, and the therapist defines his seeming masochism as mistrust ("it sounds like you don't trust my judgment"). This evokes a more genuine reaction, as the patient reveals a generally mistrustful, resentful stance, saying, in effect, that anyone who confronts him is an enemy.

In both of these examples, the therapists are trying to force the patients into more independent positions through refusing a stance of superiority and dominance. In the first case the patient, who wanted to avoid all responsibility for her problems, reacted passively to the intervention, hoping the therapist would become more assertive. In the second case the patient used masochism to avoid having to admit his deep mistrust of others and consequent rebelliousness, something his peers and the group's therapists had been pressing him to express more openly. The two patients therefore used masochistic resistance for different purposes, but in both cases the therapists' masochistic responses interfered with the resistance. In both cases the correct approach would be to continue a masochistic style with the patients until they moved to a different style of interaction.

The therapists did in fact continue their masochistic style with the two patients just discussed. The first patient endured this for three more sessions before finally becoming openly angry and attacking. This change surprised her peers, who had never before witnessed how provocative and belligerent this young woman could be. The change gave her peers a chance to see more clearly her role in the chronic battles with her mother, something the patient was slowly able to recognize and, to some extent, change in family therapy. Eventually it was learned that this patient was very uneasy about ending her role as her mother's victim, fearing that her mother had no other use for her.

The second patient became openly angry at the therapists later in the session described above, attacking them as being just as insensitive to him as his previous therapist had been. He then gave up all pretense of guilt and distress over his previous behavior. He said he felt utterly justified in how he had behaved because "adults are just assholes who'll screw you if they can. You can't trust anybody but yourself."

To summarize: the primary intervention with patients using masochistic resistance is to become masochistic oneself. Therapists must express confusion and helplessness in an attempt to avoid the role the masochistic patient needs them to play, namely the role of someone whose superiority relieves the patient of initiative and autonomy.

REFRAMING WITH ANGRY MASOCHISTIC PATIENTS

There is an additional intervention that may be used with angry masochistic adolescents: therapists may reframe the patient's masochistic productions as defiance. While the patient's words are masochistic in their actual content, therapists may respond as though the patient had been rebellious and mistrustful. (The case just discussed offers an example of this; when the patient protested he was confused, the therapist replied, "It sounds like you don't trust my judgment.") The therapist, of course, would prefer that the patient were openly mistrustful. Such a stance shows at least some acceptance of separateness and autonomy and is therefore a step beyond the masochist's fear of independence. The therapist uses reframing, therefore, to maneuver the masochistic patient toward open defiance and mistrust.

Therapists should be sure there is some fairly clear defiance in the patient's productions or attitude before they use reframing as an intervention. They ought not simply make it up or impose a defiant label on productions that are completely docile and passive. It is true, as noted earlier, that there is some indirect defiance implied even in docile masochism, but that resistance will be too far removed from the patient's experience to be useful. A patient showing traits associated with docile masochism may well be genuinely confused if the therapist tries to define the patient as mistrustful or rebellious.

It is not, however, a long step from angry masochism to open mistrust. The angry masochist feels misused and mistreated by life and others but does not feel able to complain openly about this. The angry masochistic patient therefore turns the complaints against the self in a way that frustrates and aggravates the other. Therapists can almost sense that such patients want to make an open complaint. It is not, therefore, much of a leap for therapists to define or reframe angry masochistic productions as statements of protest and mistrust.

There is a correct and an incorrect way to accomplish such reframing. The correct way is to personalize the interaction, making the therapist the target of the mistrust. The patient has avoided any genuine interaction with the therapist through a masochistic style; the therapist seeks to produce an interaction that is more promising, more genuine, and knows that an encounter that expresses anger is more genuine in this case than one expressing self-effacement. The therapist should therefore make the interaction personal—saying, in effect, "You don't trust me"—in hopes that getting the mistrust into the open will make the relationship more honest.

This personalization should be done in a neutral way, without irritation or the appearance of blame. The angry masochistic patient will expect to be blamed for wanting some measure of initiative and autonomy. If the therapist sounds critical or defensive, the patient will experience such an attitude as a rejection of his or her autonomous strivings. It may not be easy for the therapist to avoid being critical or, for that matter, angry at the patient. The angry masochistic style is frustrating and, as already noted, tends to elicit anger and sadism from others. By the time a therapist has made an effort to help the patient and seen these efforts fail due to the patient's oppressive weakness and unrelenting inferiority, it can be easy to let an intervention become contaminated with aggression, in effect blaming the patient for whatever frustration the therapist feels.

Needless to say, this is improper and probably stems from the narcissistic wound masochistic patients are so good at inflicting on their therapists. Early in this chapter I noted the way these patients make the therapist feel needed and important, only to make the therapist then feel ineffectual by failing to improve. This essentially sadistic treatment may well make the therapist angry and defensive. Sadistic intentions can easily color interventions, and the therapist may well express rejection, blame, and criticism of the patient through poorly worded interventions. This merely reinforces the patient's masochistic stance.

> A 16-year-old female had experienced truly savage abuse through-out childhood. She had developed a masochistic style over time and began during adolescence to behave in ways that were unwise and extremely dangerous. By the time she was placed in residential care, she had been raped and beaten repeatedly. Once in treatment, she defeated everyone's efforts to help her. She would agree with ob-servations about her and would agree also to ideas about how she might make progress. However, she never succeeded at anything, which was frustrating to peers and staff who tried to help. When-ever others grew aggravated and stopped trying to help, she would complain bitterly that she needed their assistance and eventually managed to get someone to try to help anew, only to fail anew. She managed to draw repeated, angry confrontations from peers on her relentless and provocative weakness. Staff decided to adopt a masochistic style themselves, hoping to force a different pattern of interaction. Several staff, however, were so angry at the patient that they had trouble keeping sadistic intentions out of their com-munications. On one occasion a group leader tried to reframe the patient's complaint that one of staff's ideas had not worked out very well. However, instead of saying, as intended, "You're pretty sure you're in the hands of people who don't know what they're doing," the staff found herself saying, "You still don't know how to trust us." Her anger at the patient had led her to cast her intervention in a critical, you're-to-blame fashion.

FURTHER CONSIDERATIONS

Patients, especially adolescent patients, can always find ways to de-feat a therapist's best efforts, and certainly this is true with maso-chistic adolescents. Masochistic youth are most likely to defeat therapy either by complaining to their parents about the therapist's protests of ineffectuality or by becoming more depressed and threat-ening self-harm.

In chapter 4 I noted that therapists should prepare the parents for interventions they might misinterpret. As anyone dealing with adolescent patients knows, it can be part of any youth's resistance to try to turn the parents against the therapist. Therapists are therefore naive or remiss (or both) if they fail to prepare the parents before beginning interventions the patient might use against them, including the interventions described in this chapter. Even if the parents do not grasp the rationale for these interventions, they will usually go along if the matter is discussed with them.

The patient has a better chance of defeating the therapist's efforts by becoming worse, that is, more depressed, perhaps suicidally so. In my judgment masochistic patients are not in fact at all likely to commit suicide, although they can engage in such forms of self-mutilation as burning themselves with cigarettes and making minor cuts on themselves. It does not matter, however, whether a masochistic patient is actually suicidal. Except perhaps for those that are most obviously fake, threats of suicide must be respected, and so, when they are made, treatment tends to revolve around them. The patient is in a position to return to a helpless position by threatening self-harm. The therapist is then maneuvered into having to treat the patient as someone who needs to be protected and assisted. The therapist has been manipulated back into the role of being superior and dominating, and the patient is again relieved of initiative and autonomy.

Finally, in my clinical experience, adolescents who show masochistic resistance do not improve significantly from antidepressant medications. This is surprising, since the predominant presenting symptom with these patients is depression. It may well be good practice to arrange a trial of such medication, but it may also be well not to expect too much. These patients are, after all, receiving secondary gain from being depressed—others do not expect much from depressed individuals, and the experience of initiative is thereby avoided. Masochistic adolescents, therefore, have good reason to stay despondent.

CHAPTER 6

PARANOID RESISTANCE

THE MISTRUSTFUL ADOLESCENT

It is generally not difficult to recognize a paranoid style in adolescent patients. Patients using this style are usually hostile, defiant, and oppositional from the outset; even those who mask their hostility initially show it quickly the first time the therapist crosses them. These patients behave in overtly rebellious, provocative, and often aggressive ways with almost every authority figure. Because of this it is often possible to recognize the paranoid style just from the presenting symptoms, even before the patient has actually been seen face to face. Mistrustful adolescents typically carry histories that suggest their poor opinion of rules and rule-makers. Their behavior is clearly rebellious and usually includes antisocial activities, behaviors that go beyond statutory offenses. Not infrequently, they have shoplifted or committed other thefts, sold drugs, and behaved aggressively with peers and even with their families. School officials usually know these adolescents well; they tend to behave in ways that lead to suspensions, or at least cause problems in the classroom by their hostile, disruptive behavior.

In sessions, paranoid youth create power struggles with the therapist and describe interactions with others that are clearly based on power struggles. They seem to invite interactions in which the other person is placed in the role of a police officer or rule-giver. Paranoid adolescents seem to want to take no responsibility for their behavior. Whatever has gone wrong is almost always the other person's fault, and this pattern holds true in sessions as well. These patients accept no responsibility for how sessions proceed. They see the session as the therapist's problem, not something between the patient and the therapist.

Their behavior is designed to thwart the therapist's best efforts, and the therapist quickly feels this, sensing that the patient will have to be dragged or carried into treatment if it is to occur. Paranoid adolescents are quick to sense when the therapist has some agenda and wants something from them, even if it is as simple as talking about the issues that led to treatment. As soon as they sense what the therapist wants or expects, they set about defeating this expectation, thereby creating a quiet (or perhaps open) struggle over who is in control.

Thus, the initial impression of the case is of an adolescent who is in conflict with every authority figure, quickly including the therapist. The patient is sullen and passively hostile or even overtly provocative in sessions and carries a history of disordered conduct or, at least, oppositional behavior, frequently leading to some encounter with the courts. The parents' complaint is that the youth is always into some trouble and that they have no control; usually the family interaction is highly charged with anger. The therapist will become aware that sessions too could easily become charged with anger.

I use the term *paranoid* to describe these patients, even though they are generally not clinically paranoid, which is to say they are not delusional and they may not so much project blame as simply reject it. Nonetheless, the dynamics are substantially paranoid, and therapists will gain insight into the case if they think in these terms. They are certainly more than simply oppositional youths who push a little beyond the limits set for them. To some extent all adolescents are oppositional and able to muster surprising amounts of righteous indignation and resentment, as can these patients but who go well beyond that. They are very active in defining adults as persons who want to force a humiliating submission, who seek to dominate them and take unreasonable advantage, and they have a paranoid's capacity to see this supposed intention behind even harmless and thoroughly ordinary interactions. Normal adolescents, even in an oppositional frame of mind, are largely protesting against the way rules impinge on their autonomy; they want the rules and rule-makers simply to leave them alone for a while. Paranoid adolescents, however, neither seek autonomy nor want to be left alone. They go out of their way to create an intense, sustained relationship, and they find it very difficult to be quiet or hidden about what they do.

One would think that individuals who were genuinely fearful and mistrustful would seek to draw as little notice as possible, like spies in a foreign land. Paranoid adolescents, by contrast, are not very secretive or reclusive. They draw attention to themselves through their behavior and attitude and cannot seem to help drawing such attention. It is true that they do keep their distance and interact in guarded ways, and so perhaps they can be thought of as secretive; yet it is just as true that they seem perpetually embroiled in highly charged exchanges with those about them and that everyone who knows them knows also what their opinions are. There is the semblance of secrecy and hiddenness and protests of wanting just to be left alone, but the reality seems to be that they insist authorities be concerned with them. Certainly it is hard to be in the office with them for very long without developing strong feelings about them; they tend to establish intense interactions.

The very noisiness of these cases distinguishes them from schizoid patients. While those adolescents adopting a schizoid adaptation may present many of the same sorts of behaviors as paranoid youth, they are hard to get hold of interpersonally and are genuinely reclusive or secretive. Their passivity and reticence are in sharp contrast to the paranoid adolescent's active attempts at creating an intense relationship with every authority figure. Even if paranoid youth do not intend to maintain the relationship, they seem to want the other to know what they think or feel; they appear to want to be known, all their protests to be left alone notwithstanding.

This suggests that these patients need the other person in some sense. I do not mean to imply that these individuals secretly have hearts of gold and just need a little understanding or love. This is an extraordinarily naive view of things, albeit one that can be found among surprising numbers of mental health professionals. Leary (1957) commented on the "common assumption that what the deprived, mistrustful person needs is love and affection" (p. 273). He suggested that mistrustful individuals are uneasy with affection and in fact feel threatened by it. Consequently, a therapist who offers love and understanding is likely to be responded to as if he or she had instead been critical or openly rejecting. Sullivan (1956) made the same point. He argued that closeness is thoroughly unnerving to paranoid individuals and usually draws an overtly defiant, mistrustful reaction.

If these patients need the other person, then, it is not to seek love and closeness. Rather, these are the people who tend to be "friendless without an enemy," as the saying goes. That is, these are individuals who are far more comfortable with conflict and deviant motives than with affiliation. They will therefore behave in ways that tend to elicit overt rejection or attempts at punishment from those around them. In fact, they cannot seem to do without this, at least not for very long.

Mistrustful adolescents are not loners; they seek relationships. Unhappily, their preferred mode of being involved with most persons—and especially with authorities—is through attitudes of resentment and bitterness. This is simply the only way they can deal with people consistently without feeling at risk. Such relationships are, of course, riddled with conflict and unstable, but it may be the instability that is attractive.

PARANOID DEPRESSION

I emphasize the point that mistrustful adolescents are not loners, because it is easy to conclude the opposite. They seem to be trying to create distance through their sour and bitter attitude. It is easy to mistake this for pain and even to try to make contact with them through speaking to this apparent pain. It is easy, in other words, to address these patients as though they were depressed and hurting and therefore in need of help. Such an approach is partly right but mostly wrong: these patients are depressed, but they are not hurting, and they do not need assistance.

Classic depression entails feeling there is something wrong with oneself; the patient feels that he or she is a bad, inferior, or damaged person. Paranoid depression, by contrast, is dysphoria built on the sense that the world is bad, that the world is an inherently disappointing place where bad things are likely to happen. Consequently, the therapist may well be correct to believe that the mistrustful adolescent is depressed, but the patient is not in pain. Rather, the patient is likely to cause pain to others. So long as the patient can do this—cause pain to others—no help is wanted, at least not by the patient.

Paranoid depression is marked by anger, accompanied by bitterness, cynicism, and fatalism. Indeed, mistrustful adolescents are typically more angry than other out-of-control youths. They seem more bothered by life and by the fairly ordinary frustrations that go with normal living than is the case with most teenagers. Certainly their experience of the world is that it is an unsatisfying place and perhaps a place where very little can be expected to last. They expect their friends to stab them in the back eventually, and they do not anticipate that dating relationships will endure either. In fact, they expect very little to work out finally. Their sense of life is that it is a disappointment, and so it is perhaps not surprising they are so angry.

In part, then, what they lay at others' feet is blame for how disappointed and angry they are at life. Life has rubbed them the wrong way, and they appear to be looking for people to take it out on. This implies, in turn that these patients need to be fighting off someone else, to be in conflict with them, or otherwise to be experiencing them as personally responsible for even a small part of their unhappiness. It is as if they are living part of their lives outside themselves, seeing the other person as intimately involved with their own well of anger. They do indeed need the other person to be part of an ever-expanding yet remarkably consistent explanation of their unhappiness. Their unhappiness is always located outside themselves, and by attacking the other person they are, in their minds, working on why they are unhappy.

It is easy to see why these patients cannot be loners, even if they seem to be trying to distance themselves from others. If they were to cut themselves off from others, they would be left alone with their anger and bitterness. They are not looking, though, for opportunities to assume responsibility for themselves but for someone else to take the responsibility, that is, to take the blame. They cannot be alone, because they need someone to blame. Paranoid depression implies relatedness, often very intense sorts of relationships, in fact.

PARANOID RELATEDNESS

Paranoid adolescents fairly broadcast their motto to everyone they meet: *it is only a matter of time until you treat me unfairly.* This is not a question or a challenge; it is, for the patient, a statement of absolute fact. Mistrustful adolescents *know* the therapist and other rule-makers want to dominate, humiliate, and coerce them. They therefore have no motivation to reveal themselves to the therapist or to cooperate in any but the most superficial fashion. They have every motivation to watch for signs that the therapist's true intentions are finally coming out, that the therapist is about to deal with them unfairly or abusively. Needless to say, they are on their guard to make sure the therapist's true intentions do not take them by surprise.

Consequently, these patients will define the therapist as a police officer, no matter how the therapist actually behaves. Mistrustful patients do indeed need the other person, but need that person to be against them, to attempt to subdue or tame them in some fashion that can both be seen through and quite possibly despised for its conventionality. It does not matter much that the other person, in this case the therapist, does not try to do any of this. These patients will experience the therapist as if he or she did.

Eventually, of course, the therapist may react to patient provocations with some limit, ultimatum, or confrontation. The therapist may be forced into such a position if a patient threatens something that is dangerous, or the patient's provocative style may eventually coerce a punitive reaction out of an irritated therapist. The mistrustful style, with its sullen, sour resentments, almost guarantees an unfavorable reaction from others sooner or later. Paranoid adolescents will seize on such a reaction as if it were the proof they had been looking for, proof that the therapist had it in mind all along to force them to submit. They will not accept the idea that they are at least partly responsible for this state of affairs. Rather, they will attribute any coerciveness or punitiveness entirely to the therapist's hidden desire to make them give in so they can be treated unfairly. They will behave in such a manner, in fact, with parents, teachers, friends, and those they date.

It is hard to escape the conclusion that it is these persons' intention to experience domination and ill will and to have to fight them off. This conclusion is not only based on the way such patients readily see betrayal everywhere but on the way that the problem almost always seems to be the other person's fault. Externalization of blame or responsibility does not of itself indicate a paranoid style, but it is part of such a style, looking to the other person as an explanation of what has gone wrong. More particularly, it is a matter of looking to the other as an explanation for one's own distress and upset.

What is lost and what is gained by doing business this way in life? What is lost is that one is never on one's own, and this is also what is gained. It is never clear whether paranoid individuals are struggling to preserve or surrender their autonomy. They seem ever to be in battle with someone else, and this suggests that they are trying to gain independence. Yet the fact that they are *always* in battle implies that they chiefly want to define themselves through being against the other, which is, of course, not independence at all, since it entails at best a negative identity, or a sense of who one is not. It appears that mistrustful adolescents can be impinged upon or taken over by even the smallest of rules or restrictions and that they can sometimes feel taken over even in the complete absence of restrictions. Anyone whose sense of separateness is so fragile is not independent (and therefore must not try to be).

Any involved or close relationship is enough to bring these issues to the forefront. This means that there are inevitable and growing fights with the parents, and it means that the structure of the classroom is bound to provoke battles. Dating relationships are problematic too, as are jobs, and of course the experience of being alone with a therapist quickly raises these issues. Any situation in which the patient is expected to adjust to someone else's rules can bring a wary, mistrustful, and eventually defiant reaction.

Shapiro (1965) makes an interesting analysis of these themes in his essay on the paranoid style. He observes that paranoid individuals avoid the experience of relaxing direct control over their intentionality and direction. Normal individuals, secure in their autonomy, can relax awareness of self-direction and give in both to their own moods and feelings and also to the will of others in most situations without feeling humiliated or threatened. This is due to their feeling competent to "go with the flow" without getting too far away from the ability to reclaim direct control if the need arises. Autonomy implies the ability to let it go, a kind of trust that one's self will be there if needed. The paranoid preference for constantly keeping a close eye on whether one is proceeding under self-direction reveals a decided insecurity about one's self, much as the need to keep a lover or friend under very tight control implies absence of trust and confidence in the relationship.

Consequently, paranoid individuals are disposed to enter into power struggles. They do not trust themselves at all and must relocate all responsibility to the other person so that they do not have to discover their own inability to be competent. The adolescent's power struggles are in fact a way of *refusing autonomy* while preserving the illusion of fighting for it. Since it is the self that is not trusted, some mechanism is needed for getting outside the question of competence quickly, which is what the power struggle does. As noted earlier, what is lost is the sense that one is on one's own, but this is also what is gained, since being on one's own would threaten to expose the patient's ineffectuality and lack of competence in life.

Neither the paranoid adult nor the mistrustful adolescent is confident of his or her competence, or the ability to handle either pleasant or unpleasant situations smoothly and spontaneously without watching carefully every step. The only difference between the adult and adolescent in this regard is that the adult tends to grow constricted and rigid in the face of doubt and insecurity, while the adolescent moves much more quickly to an impulsively aggressive response. If the adult paranoid individual gives the appearance of trying to keep the self on a short leash emotionally, the adolescent gives in to angry affect much more rapidly and puts the anger into action. Behaviors that a paranoid adult would find risky and even humiliating are indulged in by the mistrustful adolescent.

This difference is built on the psychological unsettledness of the adolescent's personality. The adult often appears to feel that there is some integrity to hold onto, and may not give in as quickly to aggressive impulses for fear of getting carried away with those feelings and, as a result, being made to look inferior. The adult, after all, lives in a larger world and is aware that there are certain expectations imposed by society. Only the most primitive or juvenile adult lets loose of the larger social context with the speed of an adolescent. The latter, by contrast, lives in a smaller segment of society and is on the margins of what is expected by the larger world. It is therefore easier to behave aggressively; the adolescent is simply not aware of how much there is to lose or, to put it in more paranoid terms, how large the danger is.

The paranoid adolescent's eagerness for power struggles is the therapist's opening. The patient does not want the burden of autonomy and the attendant threat of learning of his or her incompetence. The therapist is therefore asked to be part of the explanation for the patient's abiding unease with life by opposing or imposing on the patient. This is no small thing the patient asks, since the therapist is being assigned a key role in the patient's psychological equilibrium. In a sense, no relationship need be built up; it is there from the start.

TREATMENT OF PARANOID STYLES OF RELATEDNESS

A correct treatment approach may be arrived at through the same reasoning used with narcissistic and masochistic patients. If the patient needs the other person to play a certain type of role—in this case, to enter into a struggle over who is in control—some good can be done by refusing the role. The patient is trying to avoid being left alone with his or her anger and seeks to make the other into an explanation for the anger. The other person must consequently behave in ways that dissolve this explanation.

It is not enough simply to bypass the power struggle through proper conventional technique. The mistrustful patient will find some way to experience the therapist's comments, suggestions, or even neutrality as coercive. A therapist who keeps a proper distance and reacts with appropriate confrontations to the patient's provocations will almost certainly not be allowed this luxury. Mistrustful adolescents can experience even the most neutral, reality-based response as critical and judgmental and may even experience silence as rejection. In addition, these patients are adept at forcing the therapist to take a stand, for example, through missing sessions, "sulling up" and saying nothing at all, coming to sessions high on drugs, storming out of sessions early, or behaving at home in ways that the parents cannot tolerate.

The therapist will therefore have to adopt a style of interaction that both engages the patient and defeats the attempt to create a power struggle. The therapist's best tools for accomplishing this are, in my judgment, paradoxical interventions.

The Use of Paradox

Paradoxical interventions have been widely discussed and described in the literature (e.g.. Fisch et al. 1982, Goldberg 1973, Haley 1963, Watzlawick et al. 1974). Those familiar with this literature will realize that these interventions can be used because they provide a basis for interacting without accepting the inevitable power struggle. My own sense of this type of work, in fact, is that these interventions presuppose a power struggle and will not work in the absence of one. Given such a struggle, though, paradox offers clinicians the chance to redefine the exchange on their terms.

Haley (1986) observes that an individual who wishes to be carried about by others may be able to achieve this by authoritatively commanding them to do so; the very same thing, however, may be accomplished in just the opposite way simply by collapsing. The point to be learned is that the same goal can be pursued both by assuming all of the power but also by offering it to the other person. If we carry this lesson to the paranoid adolescent, we may respond to provocation through exerting (or trying to exert) control, or we may offer additional control to the patient.

At first glance it would seem to be a poor idea to give the patient more power. In some circumstances it most certainly would be a poor idea—for instance, if the patient were up to something dangerous or were about to attack another person. In such situations the patient truly can coerce us to take control because the consequences would simply be unacceptable if we failed to do so. However, unless matters are dangerous, giving the patient more control thwarts the paranoid project, which is built on refusing to be autonomous and making the other person into the excuse for lacking autonomy. The mistrustful patient needs the therapist to be in control; otherwise, the patient must struggle with autonomy (and the fear of being incompetent). The therapist must find some way to make the patient face just what the patient wants least to face, in this case the risks that go with autonomy, and so the strategy is to deliver to the patient the very control the patient would rather struggle over, but not possess.

There are three paradoxical interventions that are useful with mistrustful adolescents: predicting the symptom, prescribing the symptom, and reframing. Each will be discussed in turn.

Predicting the Symptom

In this style of paradox the therapist tries to guess what the patient will do in response to the therapist, the parents, or some other authority and tells the patient in advance what he or she will do. Such a prediction would have little effect were it not for the element of power struggle in the relationship. The prediction places the patient in a bind. By predicting what the patient will do, the therapist claims some control over what is happening, and if the patient in fact does what is predicted, he or she is complying, which means that the struggle has ended, at least for the moment. If the patient does not do what is predicted, the behavior is under the patient's control, and this is precisely what the patient is trying to avoid—the assumption of responsibility for his or her behavior.

Predicting a problematic behavior sidesteps the struggle for control these patients prefer. The therapist in effect is announcing a refusal to try to control and in the process leaves what might be termed a power vacuum. The only person left in control is the patient, and it may seem at first that this is what mistrustful patients wanted in the first place. As we have seen, however, it is not at all what they want; they want to battle for control, not to have it. The only way to battle with the therapist is to avoid the problematic behavior, which has the character of defiance, even though it leads to an improvement in the patient's behavior.

Predicting behavior works best in a group setting, where there is the added pressure that comes from having others available to watch. It is uncomfortable for paranoid adolescents to be viewed as predictable in such a public setting. These patients do not want to be seen as so easily understood, and they are therefore motivated to defy the prediction.

A direct prediction may be set up by a hidden prediction initially. The therapist can begin by writing on a card what the patient is expected to say or do in a session. When the expected behavior occurs, the therapist shows the card to the patient and adds a comment to the effect that the patient is predictable. In a group setting the card can be passed from patient to patient until it gets to the group member at whom it was aimed. Once this quiet prediction is accomplished, a public prediction is then added, telling the patient what is expected next in the session or before the following session.

A 16-year-old patient had been sneaking out of the house on weekends and participating in shoplifting with friends, usually followed by drug use. The father, with whom the patient lived, seldom caught his son sneaking out but would discover later what had occurred by checking his son's room and finding him gone or by checking mileage on the car. A fight would ensue, restrictions would be imposed (which would be forgotten or ignored), and the cycle would start again. The therapist noted signs that the patient was planning an escalation in his antisocial activities and began to predict this. He first predicted that the patient was thinking about a larger theft of some sort and then predicted the usual sequence between father and son. The patient became animated in denying the accusations (predictions) whereupon the therapist, also talking in a heated and excited way, bet the patient five dollars that he (the therapist) was right. One week later the therapist quizzed the father about the events of the weekend following the session and found that the patient had not sneaked out but had spent his nights watching television with the father. The therapist paid off his bet in the next session and expressed dismay at being wrong. He then accused the patient of tricking him and began a new series of predictions, leading to another heated exchange and another bet. This series of interventions succeeded in bringing the patient under better control, buying time to work with the father on setting effective limits.

In group therapy a rebellious middle adolescent was confronted on some problem and became hostile, defensive, and sullen. One of the two therapists then affected a show of irritation and dismay, cursed loudly, and leaned over to his co-therapist exclaiming, "Damnit, you were right!" He then took several dollars out of his wallet and gave it to the co-therapist, and sat back down with a disgusted look on his face. The co-therapist responded to the puzzled looks of the other group members by saying, "Am I good or what?" He then turned to the rebellious patient and somewhat contemptuously said, "You're so predictable!" The same patient was confronted again later in the group, but this time seemed unsure how to react. He actually managed to hear the other person out without becoming angry and indignant.

A patient in a residential center was confronted on an obvious rules violation and began energetically denying she had done anything. As this was a familiar pattern, one of the unit's staff had been able to prepare a three-by-five card with a prediction of this behavior. She pulled out the card and passed it to the patient, who responded first with bewilderment and then with laughter.

Prescribing the Symptom

This intervention is built on the same dynamics as predicting the symptom and is another way of bypassing the power struggle the patient seeks. In essence the therapist tells the patient to continue whatever problematic behaviors have been occurring, whether these are in or out of the therapy hour. Instead of battling the patient's resistance, the therapist goes with it, instructing the patient to do what he or she was prepared to do anyway. By refusing the power struggle in this manner, the patient is left with the decision and there is no one to oppose, hence no way to avoid autonomy. The therapist advises the patient to carry out the symptom voluntarily, willfully. This in itself makes it a deliberate act, which is what the patient was trying to avoid. Consequently, the patient is taken out of his or her comfort zone and is forced to battle the actual issue, whether to accept the risks of independence or of trying to become competent.

These prescriptions will be unexpected and will surely sound odd to the mistrustful patient, who will wonder what the therapist is up to. The therapist should therefore add an explanation, saying, for instance, that the patient is not ready to change and so should not try, or that the patient is unlikely to succeed in any attempt to change and is not strong enough to endure the failure. Whatever explanation is given should also have the character of prescribing the symptom; the explanation should say, in essence: don't change yet. The explanation should also be a little distasteful to the patient, defining the patient in terms of weakness or unpreparedness.

A different way of offering an explanation is to point out the negative consequences of change or perhaps the positive consequences of not changing. The therapist may earnestly point out that change is unsettling and anxiety-producing and that the patient may not be able to handle this. In addition, the therapist may observe that any change by the patient will bother the rest of the family, who may not be happy with the patient's current behavior but who are at least used to it and probably do not realize just how much they count on it. A combination of ingenuity and disingenuousness is needed for such explanations of just why the therapist is prescribing the very sort of problem behavior that led to treatment in the first place.

   The idea behind these interventions is to leave the patient alone, face to face with the decision how to behave. These communications give permission to be oppositional, a contradiction in terms. The effect may be compared to the effect in mathematics of multiplying one negative number by another—the equation becomes positive. In a similar way, instructing someone to be defiant sets the patient free to choose what is to be done. In my experience, the only circumstance under which prescribing the symptom utterly fails is if its use is precipitous. There must be some relationship with the patient such that the therapist has become someone to oppose or push away. If the therapist does not have this status with the patient, a prescription will have no context and will not therefore present the patient with a free choice. (By contrast, predicting the symptom can establish just such a relationship and can be used before the therapist has become someone important enough to oppose.) Used in its proper context—a power struggle—a prescription creates new options for the patient by robbing the old ones of their value.

   A 16-year-old in residential treatment had made gains that led him to questions about his formerly idealized father's fitness as a parent. Rather than face these, he regressed, becoming irresponsible with his unit chores and lying blandly when caught. Staff responded by telling him that he had come too far, too fast. They said that he needed to regress and to reassure himself by being rebellious that he was at fault, not his father. They insisted that this was what he most needed to do at that point in his treatment. When he was caught lying or being irresponsible, staff gave him the consequence of telling a certain number of additional lies over the next few hours, and they rewarded the entire unit if he met his goal. He was also given tasks on the unit with the instruction to do these in an irresponsible manner. The patient seemed nonplused by these interventions. However, he confronted his father in the next family session over being irresponsible at home and never following through with promises to do things with his son.

   In group therapy a patient had been trying to get the therapists to reassure him that they could be trusted. The therapists in turn were suspicious, reasoning that someone who was genuinely mistrustful would not trust their reassurance and therefore could not make use of it. In one session the patient was talking about physical abuse he had experienced at the hands of his father. He bitterly exclaimed that this had made him decide never to trust anyone again. The patient in actuality had a history of trusting all the wrong people and being used by them, and so the therapists were not entirely disingenuous when they told the patient that he was correct, that he should not trust anyone. They added the explanation that having such a father had kept him from learning the cues people give that allow us to know who can be trusted. He therefore should choose a cautious course and mistrust everyone. The patient was outraged and insisted the therapists were trustworthy and that he should trust them as well as his individual therapist. He declared he would show he trusted them by completing a task they had assigned some time ago that he had been resisting. The therapists continued to advise caution and to think twice before completing the assignment, while this somewhat paranoid young man vigorously argued that he should trust more people.

Prescribing the symptom may not go smoothly. The session may become charged with tension and upset on the part of the patient, who is, after all, seeking some sort of angry struggle. Just because the therapist is refusing such a struggle, the patient will not automatically welcome the situation. Indeed, the patient may even switch sides, insisting the therapist take a different position. The therapist's prescription offers the patient the chance to carry out a willful act; by switching sides, the patient refuses this chance and in effect asks the therapist if the power struggle cannot be resumed. Again, the patient seeks to escape making an independent decision or tries to avoid assuming responsibility.

The patient described in Chapter 2 (pp. 45–47) illustrates this point. The patient had spent much time and energy trying to make her mother's life miserable, although the patient herself had wound up paying quite a price. The therapist suggested that the patient's approach made a lot of sense and that it must have brought her much satisfaction; he proposed that she continue trying to "get" her mother and offered to help her come up with new ways to do it. Immediately the patient changed sides and began to list all the ways her strategy had actually hurt her. She then insisted she loved her mother and should not have hurt her in the ways she did. For most of the session, the patient energetically made the very points the therapist might have made. She ended with a forceful argument that she ought to change.

Patients switch sides in order to renew the struggle. If they must oppose someone, the actual position does not matter as much as the fact that the other person does not also hold the position. However, patients are in a bind in such a situation. While switching sides brings them into conflict with the therapist's prescription, it makes them comply with broader, adult standards and ways of looking at events. In the case just mentioned, the patient resumed her struggle with the therapist but wound up complying with points her mother had made to her earlier in the session (before the therapist met with the patient alone).

This is an unstable situation. Mistrustful patients cannot typically switch sides and stay there. The therapist should seek to promote the instability. The therapist may, for instance, advise the patient to switch back to the original position as soon as the session ends or predict that this will happen. It is best if the prescription or prediction can be made in the presence of others, either group members or family. The idea is to make patients struggle with themselves rather than with the therapist. Prescriptions do this by highlighting behaviors that had previously been automatic or reflexive, thereby making them more conscious and deliberate. When patients switch sides, they plainly have not consciously chosen to do so; it is another reflexive act. Continuing to make paradoxical prescriptions, then, and doing this in the presence of people who know the patient, elevates the problem out of the realm of what can be done automatically. The patient has to think about it, and the simple fact that there are others involved makes it a certainty that this will happen. Therefore the therapist should continue to be paradoxical even after the patient switches to a desired stance.

Not every prescription leads to a tense exchange; it is possible to bring humor into sessions when prescribing a symptom. At times patients will find their own behavior so ludicrous they cannot help laughing when the therapist prescribes (and thereby describes) it. The appearance of humor is a good sign. It implies a willingness to be spontaneous, to let down one's guard, and go with the mood of the moment. It implies a surrender and an abandonment of a tight, embattled perspective in which control is the order of the day. Usually humor by the patient means that matters are changing for the better. Patients can surrender (in this case to humor) only after they become more confident that they can always regain control of themselves; in turn, they can have this confidence only if they feel competent, which is to say autonomous.

> A patient in a residential center had made no progress in two months. Her favorite maneuver was to mess up some unit-wide activity, making all of her peers angry at her, whereupon she would assume an indignant, wounded, and belligerent posture. She was given the paradoxical task of trying to interfere with at least three unit-wide activities daily, and her peers were instructed to criticize her vigorously if she failed. Before the patient had gotten through the second day of this assignment, she was plainly enjoying herself and making it into a game. She would loudly announce that "I'm about to screw this up!" Her peers would then watch and applaud as she did so. The interaction in fact became playful and fun for the whole unit, and the patient gained a place within the group rather than on its outskirts. All staff agreed that the week that followed was by far the patient's most productive week since admission.

Prescribing the symptom may also be used when the therapist wants to regain control of a patient who is moving out of control. Using prescription in this way does not address the issue of autonomy and so probably does little to undermine resistance. However, the mistrustful adolescent can at times reduce therapy to a matter of trying to contain wild and rebellious behavior, and it is a help to have some tools that may be used for this purpose. In this situation the therapist must put the patient in a bind such that to get out of the bind the patient must pursue the goal that was originally what the therapist (or parent) wanted.

This use of paradox entails contingency. In essence the patient is offered a chance to do what the therapist (or parent) originally wanted but at the price of accomplishing a distorted and exaggerated version of what the patient wanted. Perhaps this is variation on the old saying, "Be careful what you wish for—you might get it." In this case the patient is given a version of what he or she wanted but in a way that is aversive. The price of being freed from this situation is compliance with what was originally asked, although usually with some additional price tacked on. Such an intervention works only if the therapist has the power to enforce it or if the therapist and parents are willing to run the risk that the patient will decide to accept the exaggerated version of what he or she wanted.

A late adolescent patient threatened to run away from home. His parents replied that he would be thrown out of the house with all of his belongings if he could not persuade them within twenty-four hours not to do this.

A patient in residential treatment turned 18, the age at which he could sign out of treatment in his state. He began threatening to do this. In reply he was told he would be discharged before the week was up unless he could offer compelling reasons to be allowed to remain.

A patient in a hospital program refused to get out of bed in the morning. She was told she would not be allowed to get out of bed for at least six hours and if she failed to arise then would not get another chance for an additional six hours, and so on. Six hours later the patient was bored and wanted to get up. She was allowed to do so only after she agreed to do extra chores on the unit for the patients who were first out of bed that day.

A therapist met with a new adolescent group for the first time. The patients were not well motivated, and several of the patients sat as a subgroup, making disruptive comments and noises. The therapist praised them for mastering their anxiety in that manner and ordered them to continue to make disruptive comments whenever they felt frightened. He then told the rest of the group to tolerate this disturbance because the patients truly needed the release. The disruptive patients were baffled and grew very quiet, even after the therapist instructed them several times to be disruptive. He finally labeled their quietness as defiance and rebellion and seemed frustrated he could not induce disruptive comments from them as other patients started trying to work.

Reframing and Relabeling

Reframing and relabeling are interventions designed to change the way a patient's behavior is seen or experienced. The two terms are often used interchangeably, but there is a subtle difference. Reframing changes the frame of reference, while relabeling uses a new word or phrase to describe the patient, producing a different connotation. The frame of reference is changed by finding a larger or smaller context for what is happening—for instance, moving an event from a family context to a purely intrapsychic focus. Relabeling occurs when the therapist finds a different implication in an event than what others experience and then finds a new term to capture that implication.

The idea behind this intervention is to bring patients into conflict with themselves rather than with an outside authority. The new framework or label should reveal to patients some motive or intent of which they were unaware that is at odds with their conscious purpose. Thus it is their own conscious intentions that suddenly are at odds with their behavior, not the desires of an external authority. By wrestling with themselves, they move away from fighting with the therapist (or parents) for autonomy and move closer to fighting with themselves over what to do, which is an aspect of autonomy.

Even if patients are not prepared to struggle with themselves and thereby learn something about autonomy, reframing and relabeling may be useful in bringing the patient's behavior under control, much as with the use of prescription for the same purpose. While the therapist appears to be empathically understanding the patient, in fact the therapist is putting the patient in a bind. The therapist appears to be taking the patient seriously, but what is "uncovered" in the process is designed to make the patient's behavior untenable.

A 14-year-old refused to go to school, bringing his divorced parents into intense conflict over what to do and eventually causing the county's juvenile court to threaten legal action against them. The mother begged the father to come to the house and make the boy get out of bed and attend school. The father, however, was afraid of his son and would not do more than tell him on the phone that he ought to go to class. The patient developed a nearly psychotic protectiveness toward his mother and insisted he did not dare leave the house because other boys in the neighborhood might break in to rob or rape his mother. The therapist believed the patient was paranoid and was projecting his own incestuous and sadistic fantasies onto the other neighborhood boys. The therapist believed the patient wanted his father to assert his dominance to offer protection from such fantasies. The patient, however, sensed the father's weakness and dared not make a test of wills, afraid he would beat the father and thereby lose his only buffer from the unwanted fears and wishes. Consequently the therapist decided to reframe the situation and told the patient it was clear he was trying to communicate that he missed his father and wanted to see more of him. The therapist insisted if the patient could not return to school, they needed to have sessions with the father "so you can tell him what you feel." The patient returned to school the next week rather than face such sessions. Returning to school also got the patient away from his mother most of the day, relieving the intensity of the young man's feelings.

A patient had been intimidating other members of a therapy group, making them afraid to say anything to him that might anger him. They saw him as strong and formidable, even though he was not especially muscular or large. Some members openly admitted being scared of him, and the patient proudly talked of how fearsome he was, glorying in his macho image. The therapists decided to relabel the patient. They told him in the presence of the group that in their experience "boys your age act like this when they are afraid of their mothers, or of their feelings about their mothers." They refused to elaborate their meaning, but other group members suddenly began to see this patient as weak and tied to his mother, effectively taking away his power over the group.

A middle adolescent patient was quite wild and rebellious, behaving in ways that were unimaginable to his staid, conservative, middle-class parents. The patient was aware of the discrepancy between his wild behavior and his parents' conservatism and experienced himself as dismissing his parents. The therapist told him he was actually being loyal to his father and showing how much he was still tied to him. He said that the patient had picked up his father's unconscious desire to "run free" and be rid of responsibility and was acting out his father's fantasies so "your old man can experience them vicariously." The therapist then expressed concern that the patient was at an age when he should be breaking free of his parents, not acting out their fantasies for them. In this relabeling, the patient was given a way of experiencing his behavior that was precisely the opposite of what he intended.

FURTHER CONSIDERATIONS

In the preceding discussion on the use of paradox I have commented that the therapist at times is trying to maneuver the mistrustful patient into behaving autonomously but is at other times simply trying to control or contain the patient. What the therapist wants, of course, is to confront the paranoid patient with autonomy. What the therapist most certainly does not want is to have to control the patient, since this plays into the patient's style of resistance. Unhappily, working with these patients probably entails both autonomy and containment, it being quite rare to find a mistrustful patient who never has to be controlled by the therapist and who is always available for the kind of work that restores autonomy.

One of the virtues of paradoxical interventions is that they allow the therapist to go through the inevitable periods of having to control the patient without doing so as an authority. The therapist is indeed working at changing the patient's behavior and bringing symptoms under adult control, but this work is always disguised as something else. Thus, the therapist can go about this part of the treatment without getting solidly into a police officer's role with the patient. When the therapist is forced to try to exert direct control over behavior, the mistrustful patient is gratified; the therapist has fit into the role that complements the patient's rebelliousness, and it is subsequently harder to get back to a stance that forces the patient to move toward independence and competence. Consequently, when therapists find themselves having to contain an acting-out, mistrustful adolescent, paradoxical techniques should be tried first.

In addition to addressing the issue of autonomy through paradox, the therapist may try to raise this subject more or less directly. It is unlikely the patient will be able to tackle this subject, at least at first. It may be possible, though, to raise the topic and at least draw the patient's interest to his or her underlying motivation. If the therapist wants to attempt such a thing, it is best to make a cryptic remark on the subject. For instance, if the patient relates a recent argument at home or at school, the therapist may respond with a comment about the patient's fear of being found inept or incompetent. This comment will seem completely off the subject and may thereby attract the patient's interest, leading in a useful direction. Or the therapist might systematically react to reports of any argument or conflict as if the patient had related being afraid of autonomy. This sort of cryptic response may arouse the patient's interest, leading to discovery of the issues that underlie the mistrustful style.

The therapist can tell the resistance phase is concluding when mistrustful patients are willing to admit their responsibility in some conflict. When the patient does this, the therapist should take it seriously and at least for the moment abandon paradoxical or cryptic interventions. Therapists may have a clue that some change is underway if they find themselves not feeling pulled toward a struggle during sessions. If the patient is not trying to draw the therapist into a conflict, it is a sign that conflicted relationships are not so necessary to the patient's equilibrium and therefore that the resistance phase of treatment is ending.

CHAPTER 7

THE SCHIZOID DEFENSE

THE PRESENTING PICTURE

Use of the term schizoid tends to be confusing. For instance, some of the early object relations theorists, including Fairbairn (1952) and Guntrip (1969, 1971) appear to use this term to describe patients who would today be considered borderline personalities, while other writers (e.g., Laing 1960) bring the category very close to schizophrenia. The common ground in all descriptions, however, is that the schizoid patient is afraid of or at least terribly conflicted about contact with other people. Consequently, the hallmark of the schizoid patient is an uneasy relationship with others, characterized either by shy, fearful withdrawal or by cold detachment. These are patients who want to keep their distance and avoid needing another person.

To be sure there are decided differences between adult schizoid patients and adolescents using the schizoid defense, and these differences will be explored later in this chapter. They have in common, though, a tortured relationship to the social world, the world of other human beings. Adolescent patients using the other forms of resistance discussed in this book come to therapy wanting something from other people; the mistrustful patient, for instance, wants an enemy, and even the narcissistic adolescent wants someone to sustain the illusion of his or her value. By contrast, the patient using the schizoid adaptation is trying hard not to need anything from others, except possibly to be left alone.

The patient's presenting symptoms are not likely to help with diagnosis; symptoms tend to be the usual complaints brought by (or about) out-of-control adolescents, a mixture of behavior problems, drug use, and disturbed mood—in this case, the appearance of depression. Even the patient's relationships do not at first glance seem especially different from what is found with other out-of-control patients. Relationships are highly conflicted and frequently seem dominated by anger, much as with mistrustful adolescents.

With further study, however, the therapist will begin to notice significant differences in spite of the apparent similarities. It is true that the schizoid adolescent, like other out-of-control youths, frequently establishes anger-driven relationships. Yet the schizoid adolescent uses anger to create distance, to erect walls and barriers to further contact, while the mistrustful patient, for instance, uses anger precisely as the form of relatedness. Similarly, the schizoid adolescent typically uses drugs and alcohol fairly heavily, much as do other out-of-control patients. The schizoid adolescent, however, tends to use alone, which is in very sharp contrast to most drug-abusing youths, who usually are drawn into contact with others by their drug use. Even disordered conduct is driven by different motives; while other adolescents behave in antisocial ways as an expression of entitlement and/ or defiance, schizoid patients tend to engage in such behavior in order to act out fantasies, typically escapist fantasies of not caring (about a would-be caretaker's rules) or not needing anyone's approval.

At every point schizoid adolescents and other out-of-control youths seem to cross paths, closer study shows that the schizoid patient has different intentions. Even though the actual behavior looks the same, schizoid adolescents are trying to declare a certain independence from the world of others. They are not related to those about them except in a formal, going-through-the-motions sort of way. These patients usually have few if any friends—not even "drug buddies." In sessions this detachment may lead the therapist to feel bored and alone, even though the patient may be talking freely at the time. As it becomes increasingly clear that the patient is not especially involved with or interested in friends, family, and for that matter the therapist too, the possibility of schizoid resistance should be considered.

SCHIZOID DEPRESSION

Depression is likely to be a component of the presenting picture, and yet this is certainly not depression in the usual sense of the term. It may not be entirely accurate to say that these patients are unhappy, but they plainly lack happiness. Therapists may not see the presence of painful affect so much as the absence of aliveness. There is an abiding emotional flatness to these patients, punctuated by periods of anger or hostility, almost as if they arouse themselves to drive others away and then sink back into a kind of emotional vacancy. There is little emotion, little humor, little curiosity. Mood seems suppressed as much as depressed.

The chief characteristic of this type of depression is apathy. Apathy is the absence of connectedness with the outside world, a failure to become interested or invested. The normal state of human beings is to interact with the world around them, to reach out hopefully to engage the world and pull some response that will first define and then sustain the sense of self. The schizoid adaptation is in retreat from this normal state of affairs and seeks to quit interaction with the world by avoiding interest in it. Apathy, or the absence of feeling, levels the emotional landscape, since no event is experienced as significant or important. Perhaps there is even a kind of triumph to being able to reduce all events to the same insignificant status.

It is impossible to be apathetic without being at the same time in retreat from the world, particularly the world of others. Consequently, the apathetic individual tends to be fantasy-ridden. When placed in circumstances that others would find crushingly boring and void of stimulation, these individuals tend to be relatively untroubled. They are detached from the outside world anyway and find it easy to lose themselves in fantasy. While these fantasies may have some exciting and stimulating content, it is just as likely that they are drifting, essentially empty fantasies. Schizoid adolescents can get lost in private reverie states and deep daydreams that approach dissociative episodes. When pressed on what they were thinking about, they will often admit they were thinking about nothing at all and were simply somewhere else. The important thing for the schizoid patient is not to fantasize about something in particular but, rather, not to be thinking about the world at hand.

This sort of detachment from external reality tends to empty the emotional life—hence the drifting and empty quality to the schizoid depression. Such patients can seem emotionally dead, passively going through the motions of daily activities in a somewhat robotic way. They almost seem to merge with whatever inanimate or human environment they find themselves in, letting that environment provide all of their energy and direction (Kernberg 1975). There is a hollow quality to them, an emptiness and aloneness that is hard to penetrate or to fill with one's own presence. Even their drug use tends to be of the sort that produces a drifting, mellow state of mind; they use marijuana or inhalants, but usually not cocaine, amphetamines, or hallucinogens.

If the chief mental characteristic of the schizoid depression is apathy, then its interpersonal correlate is passivity. The passive stance is to take no action, make no deliberate move. Such a stance reflects the sense of futility that typifies the schizoid state of mind. If nothing can change, then action is futile, and the very best that can be expected from purposeful action is that it will be ineffectual. Consequently, there is no point to action or to becoming invested in trying to impact the world. Passivity denies the importance of a world that is felt to be uninfluenceable anyway. Indeed, passivity makes the other person insignificant and eventually unreal.

The individual using a schizoid defense relies on passivity to enter a state of mind in which neither the self nor the world is taken seriously. It appears that the patient is trying to believe (or has succeeded in believing) that nothing matters, that nothing will come of events. Schizoid adolescents can engage in behavior that is grossly dangerous with little apparent concern.

One high school sophomore would walk on railroad tracks at night while listening with headphones to a portable tape player at full volume. He seemed unconcerned with the danger, and his peers had the impression that the danger was completely unreal to him.

Similarly, schizoid adolescent patients engaged in dangerous drug practices appear oblivious to unwanted consequences in a way that goes beyond denial: they truly believe that whatever consequences may come of events have nothing to do with them, that it is all somehow unreal. This is the true result of passivity, I believe: to induce an experience of the world such that it and the self are unreal.

Time is static in this state of mind. In the future, nothing changes, which is another way of saying that everything is futile, that there is no hope or even any purpose in trying to hope. Such a static experience of time is another way of making events unreal. Events are real if they have an impact, and the consequences of an event are the chief means by which it impacts us. However, consequences exist in the future; they are what *will* occur. If the present moment is static, or (perhaps better) stagnant, then the future feels like an abstracted irrelevancy. Consequences are therefore irrelevant as well, and events are not real. The schizoid experience of time goes hand in hand with other elements of schizoid depression to support emotional deadness, apathy, and passivity.

Among the different types of resistance shown by out-of-control adolescents, the schizoid defense is the one most likely, in my judgment, to lead to suicide. There are other types of depression in out-of-control patients, but they are not as likely to lead to self-destructive behavior. The narcissistic patient may become deflated, but in general these youths think too highly of themselves to attempt self-harm. Masochistic patients are certainly depressed and at times deeply miserable, but this is a stable condition, not one from which they typically seek escape; indeed, masochistic patients seem comfortable with their distress. Mistrustful adolescents can be depressed, but they externalize the cause of the depression. If they seek to harm anyone, it will be the person they see as responsible for their unhappiness. Finally, as we will see in the next chapter, affectively labile adolescents may harm themselves, but not in an attempt to die. They seek to demonstrate incompetence and neediness (in a fashion similar to masochistic patients) in order to induce the other to take care of them.

By contrast, the schizoid depression leaves little reason to live. The world has been reduced to unreality, and consequently so has the self. There is little left to tie the individual to the world. If the resulting aloneness and emotional deadness become burdensome, death may seem desirable.

> The youth mentioned earlier who walked on railroad tracks at night was eventually killed by a train. Those who had known him recalled that he kept to himself at school, had no friends, and usually slept through classes. His peers occasionally reached out to him, and he had been pleasant to them, yet uninvolved. No one seemed surprised at his death. He had effectively conveyed to his peers that he saw no point in trying.

THE SCHIZOID ADOLESCENT COMPARED WITH THE SCHIZOID ADULT

Adult schizoid pathology is characterized by three traits: the false self system; excessive self-consciousness; and disembodiment. By contrast, adolescents showing a schizoid defense typically show only disembodiment, even though they have traits that seem to serve purposes similar to those served by the false self system and self-consciousness. We will learn more about the adolescent patient and that patient's difference from the schizoid adult by discussing these three characteristics.

The False Self System

A number of writers (Guntrip 1969, Laing 1960, Winnicott 1960/ 1965) have developed the concept of a false self system. Quickly stated, the false self is the schizoid individual's way of dealing with the outside world, a world that is experienced as unable to acknowledge or accept the patient as he or she actually is. The schizoid solution is to dissociate private wishes, feelings, and intentions and instead offer an ingenuine but automatic compliance with the wishes of others. At first glance it may seem that this is an attempt to fit in, to win acceptance or perhaps some standing in the world of others, but such is not the patient's intent. Rather, the intent is to hide from others any sign of caring about making an impact on them. The false self is intended to mask self-assertiveness and willfulness from a world that is (experienced as) unwilling to accommodate the individual's autonomous strivings. The intent is to protect the individual's authentic or true self from an unresponsive world.

Several writers (Giovacchini 1979, Laing and Esterson 1964, Segal 1964) have noted the "good child" qualities shown by schizoid patients as they grew up. The parents remember these patients as especially compliant children, who did not seem to mind the restrictions and limitations imposed by the parents or the world at large, as if they were more than willing to surrender their own preferences in favor of what was asked or required by the environment.

This pathological compliance reveals the abandonment of the child's autonomous strivings. While most children effect a series of more or less satisfactory compromises between what they want and what the world will allow, schizoid individuals become a passive imprint of the demands of others, jettisoning their private wishes. This compliance does not reflect their true feelings but rather the false self. True and false self are therefore terms that describe the individual's "freedom (or the lack of it) to be spontaneous and genuine in experiencing his or her feelings, wishes, and intentions, and in presenting these to the world" (Sherwood and Cohen 1994, p. 51). When we speak of the false self, we are referring to the way an individual's genuine wishes are replaced with mechanical conformity to external reality.

The problems with this solution are obvious. To begin with, the false self, by lying between the individual and reality, impoverishes the true self and makes both the world and the individual seem manufactured or fake. Perception and action both feel unreal, creating a sense of alienation and futility. In addition, dependency on others must be avoided. Dependency would entail revealing genuine needs and feelings, which in turn would threaten the hidden true self; perhaps even more important, it was dependency (as an infant on a presumably unempathic caretaker) that led to the need to protect the true self in the first place. Dependency is therefore experienced as dangerous, thereby restricting relationships to formal and detached interactions, sustaining the sense of estrangement and aloneness.

Unlike the schizoid adult, the adolescent using the schizoid defense does not, in my opinion, show a false self system. The hallmark of this system is, after all, compliance with the wishes of others (Laing 1960, Winnicott 1960/1965), but the out-of-control adolescent can hardly be described as compliant. The patient's presenting symptoms generally include behaviors that are defiant, illegal, or at the very least contrary to parental wishes.

In place of compliance, the adolescent offers *passivity* when confronted with demands from the outside world. I discussed passivity earlier, describing it as a means of neutralizing the impact others might make on the patient and suggesting that the eventual result of thoroughgoing passivity is to make the self and the world seem unreal. Passivity strips away energy, initiative, and autonomy. It thereby achieves much the same purpose as the false self system, which is also trying to mask evidence of autonomous strivings.

Since we are concerned here with treatment issues, it is best to focus on the interpersonal consequences of passivity as an adolescent alternative to the false self system. If we remember that the purpose of the false self is to protect the true self, then we may reason that the purpose of passivity is also to protect the patient. But from what exactly? It appears to me that other people are the problem for the adolescent using the schizoid defense. Others—if not neutralized— are potentially exciting, and the patient begins to want the aliveness and pleasure that can come from having others in one's life. Passivity avoids engagement with others and enforces aloneness. It is difficult to become excited by another person from a passive position.

Passivity takes the individual into fantasy. In normal life, we are sustained emotionally by interactions with the real world, usually the world of people. Passivity, however, buffers the world's impact and makes other people sufficiently vague that their influence on us becomes scattered and without focus. If the world of others is thereby neutralized, it is possible to drift mentally, to rely on fantasy more than reality. Schizoid adolescents do not necessarily have a dramatic fantasy life (though they may) but the impact of fantasy is greater than the impact of external reality, even if the fantasies are banal.

The schizoid adolescent lives in a kind of drifting, fantasy-based world, insulated from the enlivening influence of others. In such a state no ambition is expressed, nor drive or persistent intention. As with the false self system, the aim is to protect (i.e., hide) willfulness or self-assertion by cutting it off from whatever might excite autonomous strivings.

Self-Consciousness

Adult schizoid patients are characterized by painful self-consciousness, or "an awareness of oneself as an object of someone else's observation" (Laing 1960, p. 113, emphasis deleted). To be self-conscious is to assume that others take much more notice than in fact is likely, and it is easy to conclude that such people may actually wish to be seen by others, that this is perhaps an important means of being reassured that one is alive and real. However, this wish is a sword that cuts both ways. On the one hand, if I feel unsure of my reality and autonomous identity, it may be a help to be seen by others, since this means I am here after all. On the other hand, since I feel unsure of my autonomous identity, the other's gaze is threatening; it pins me down and can perhaps evacuate me of all definition except whatever definition the other person wishes to bestow.

There is therefore both a *need* to be seen and a *fear* of being seen in schizoid patients. Being seen brings a sense of reality. While the patient's own feelings and intentions are vague and ill-defined, the other's intentions, by contrast, seem imperative. Known by and conformed to the other, the schizoid patient feels validated or defined, and yet the definition is not a comfortable one. The schizoid individual feels transparent before the other person's gaze and robbed of whatever identity he or she may have had: "Not being seen by others brings a sense of drifting unreality or depersonalization, while being seen can be experienced as immobilization and penetration by an overpowering, alien reality" (Sherwood 1987, p. 164).

The danger in the other person's gaze is the schizoid patient's vulnerability to shame. Phenomenologically, shame is the sense that I am fraudulent and that this may be seen by others (Charles P. Cohen, in Sherwood 1987). These patients are vulnerable to shame because of their sense that the world is unlikely to accept them as they are— hence their attempts to hide their own intentions and feelings be- hind the false self system, as described earlier. When they enter into relationships, however, they feel that they have kept something from the other person (namely, the true self). Although schizoid patients are not aware of what they are trying to hide, they nonetheless know there is something they are keeping hidden. They fear that this might become known and that the other person could then despise them for their deceit. Thus, every relationship is experienced as having been built on fraudulence. This fear that fraudulence can be discovered at any moment is the root of the schizoid individual's painful self-consciousness.

These dynamics do not hold for the adolescent using the schizoid defense, however. In my experience, such adolescents do not dem- onstrate painful self-consciousness or a tendency to feel ashamed. Some of the things these patients say and do would certainly make a schizoid adult feel self-conscious (they would also make a normal adult feel this way), but the adolescent showing schizoid resistance is not similarly burdened. The difference between the adult and the ado- lescent is that the latter does not feel defined by the other's gaze. The adult reacts as though the look of the other had the power to petrify and deaden. Freedom from this power comes from being inaccessible to the other, presenting the false self to the other person. The ado- lescent also wants to be inaccessible to others, but not for the same reason. The adolescent hopes to avoid emotional arousal, coming to life, or getting his or her hopes up.

The problem for the adolescent is much the same as for the adult, but matters have not gone as far. The problem is still other people. For the true schizoid individual the problem is how to deal with people without being deadened by their gaze on the one hand or by the false self system that is used to defend against their gaze on the other hand. The adolescent who uses the schizoid defense is not so vulnerable to the other's gaze or to the other's reality. But the adolescent is vulner- able to the disappointment the other brings. It has been the youth's experience that the social world is utterly treacherous and difficult to negotiate, that wanting anything from others leads to problems. For some such youths, it turns out that the problem is engulfment or being taken over by the other person, much as with the true schizoid individual. For other adolescents, the problem is that too much is wanted from others, who are therefore unlikely to give what is wanted. In this case the individual feels perpetually let down and rejected, and the solution is to be done with people. In either case the schizoid defense is an attempt to construct the world in ways that insulate the individual from needing other people. Being solitary seems better.

Like the true schizoid patient, then, the adolescent who shows a schizoid style of resistance wants to be inaccessible to others, to be unmoved by them. These patients' passivity is a tool for this. Passivity renders the patient virtually invisible interpersonally. The true schizoid might wish to be invisible, not to be seen by the other and thereby captured by the other's gaze. The adolescent achieves some measure of invisibility through refusing to be engaged or impacted (passivity). If involvement with others simply leads to disappointment, something is needed that will deny the importance of the other person. Passivity accomplishes this by saying, in effect, that others are not worth the effort. As noted earlier, passivity makes the other person insignificant and eventually unreal. It also makes the patient invisible or unknowable, which is the correlate of the true schizoid individual's excessive self-consciousness.

Disembodiment

Winnicott (1960/1965) made the observation that the true self is rooted in the "aliveness of the body tissues and the working of the body functions" and noted too that the very idea of the true self "does no more than collect together the details of the experience of aliveness" (p. 148). The true self has its origins as "the summation of sensorimotor aliveness" (p. 149). These observations confirm what we all intuitively know, that to be human is to be embodied. There is a genius to the vision produced by Jewish and early Christian apocalyptic writers that the dead would rise from their graves at the Day of Judgment, in contrast to the more schizoid Greek idea that any life after death would involve the soul only. It is hard to conceive of human life without thinking of the human body.

The body is the seat of self-image, emotion, aliveness, and drive. It is not the sum total of such things, but it is the soil from which they grow and in the decline of which they eventually wither. Of course, emotion, aliveness, and such run counter to the schizoid project. They leave the schizoid individual (like the rest of us) vulnerable to all that can go wrong when we want something from life. The body therefore is the seat of vulnerability and something to be disavowed in the schizoid approach to life.

Disembodiment is a means of organizing experience so that the body is simply one thing among other things in the world. Instead of being the locus of the self, the body is reduced to the status of an object, something to be seen, dealt with, and maneuvered about, but not the center of one's existence. The schizoid patient tries to split the body off from self-experience. Of course this is a virtually impossible project, but a project that one can make some progress along nonetheless. The body is observed almost as if it belonged to some other person, regarded with as much detachment as the patient can muster. Very often we notice that such patients move somewhat stiffly and awkwardly. Some such patients sometimes move very little, in fact; I have never met a schizoid patient of any age who was an athlete.

Adolescents using the schizoid defense share this trait with true schizoid individuals. Both are disembodied, or attempting to live a purely mental, fantastic existence. The adolescent may express this in very different ways than the true schizoid patient. The adolescent frequently expresses disembodiment through behaviors that reveal or imply a disregard for the body. Female patients, for instance, may have a history of sexual promiscuity and yet have experienced very little sexual pleasure from such behavior. Often these patients will report having simply "gone somewhere else" during intercourse, meaning that they dissociated themselves from the experience. Both male and female patients will report having placed themselves in dangerous situations without having really experienced it as dangerous, even when danger overtook them. Finally, some patients use self-mutilation either to prove their disdain for the body or to try to bring some sense of being alive through evoking pain or the sight of blood.

One 15-year-old with a history of sexual promiscuity was at a loss to explain her behavior. She initially said that "getting laid gave me a sense of power and importance." Her therapist pointed out that she had surely noticed it was not difficult to arouse an adolescent male sexually and that there could not be too much artistry or triumph to such a thing. The patient replied that she was aware of this but that she had not been able to think of any other reason she "slept around so much." She went on to realize (somewhat later) that the triumph and power she had felt after sex had been triumph over herself, not over her partner.

Several months into treatment and after making progress, this same patient described having once been with friends when a gang-related fight broke out. She had been chased and shot at and was in what sounded like a very dangerous situation. After making her escape, she went to the house of a casual friend and before the night was over had been beaten up and raped. The patient said she was bringing up these events because she was puzzled at not having been afraid when she was shot at and at not being especially troubled over being raped. She was in fact dismayed and worried by the fact that "it didn't seem that important at the time. I mean, I knew I could get hurt, but it didn't upset me."

These sorts of behaviors may occur with other out-of-control adolescents, but their experience of them will be different from the schizoid experience. Adolescents using the schizoid defense will be indifferent or detached, even though they are in situations that would induce strong and even extreme emotions in most persons. Disembodiment is above all an attempt to be done with strong emotion, however, and so it is not surprising that the patient just described managed to feel very little while she was being shot at and later as she thought about it. Being rid of the body means being rid of spontaneity and therefore being able to stay in control of the ways the world has an impact.

THE SCHIZOID DEFENSE

In light of the preceding studies, we can sketch the underlying clinical picture of the adolescent who uses schizoid resistance. We can start with other people, who are simply too much for the patient to manage. Either they overwhelm the self and threaten to take over or, more typically, they threaten to make the patient hopeful of being loved and cared for. Others are dangerous on either account, and this brings the patient to want to be left alone. Life becomes a series of maneuvers to accomplish this and to quiet any longings for intimacy with others. The adolescent uses passivity, being interpersonally inaccessible and even invisible, and disembodiment to avoid the perils of the human world.

I have referred to this as the schizoid *defense*, a term used first by Laing (1960). But a defense against what? In answering, we must keep in mind that we are not discussing true schizoid individuals but adolescents who are showing elements of a schizoid style. We are therefore discussing patients who are more accessible than they might wish to be and who can be led to hope in varying degrees. Whatever schizoid trends we see are more mutable than with true schizoid patients. The fact that these patients can be reached makes it important to know what they defend against.

First of all, the patient is defending against reality. Above all else, schizoid traits manage to make both self and the world unreal. It is a way of living without feeling alive. But in order to accomplish what? This question can be answered in several different ways. The patient hopes to avoid strong affect, since affect can sweep us away and is therefore dangerous to someone who wants not to be impacted or influenced. The patient also hopes to avoid dependency, since dependency might awaken need of others and, as the patient sees it, inevitable, crushing disappointment. Finally, the patient hopes to avoid hope, since hope implies vulnerability to the future. Since contact with reality is necessarily mediated, in part, by affect, dependency, and hope, we can conclude that the patient is trying to shut down and negate reality.

We must, however, answer the question in another way. It is certainly true that the schizoid defense is aimed at reality, but this simply begs the question. What makes an unreal world preferable? The real world threatens to awaken something in the patient that he or she would rather keep quiet: self-assertion. It is not external reality that is the problem so much as an internal reality, the desire to express wishes and needs and impose these on the world without undue fear. It is not, of course, really possible to separate inner and outer reality in this way; self-assertion implies a world external to the individual's subjective reality. However, I am making this distinction in order to emphasize that there is a particular type of self-experience the patient is trying to avoid.

In Chapter 3, I suggested that the underlying or core pathology with out-of-control adolescents was a type of narcissistic disturbance, an effort at maintaining the perfection of mother–infant fusion. With patients who are drawn toward the schizoid defense, this underlying or core pathology takes an unusual turn, a turn that makes self-assertion especially problematic. To understand the situation we should start with normal development, with the well-known and much studied *rapprochement* conflict over staying close to the mother or becoming psychologically separate. The healthy child gradually pursues separateness, altering the relationship with the mother by both pulling away and protesting at the same time. In narcissistic pathology the child does not successfully pull away. Rather, the verdict goes to closeness with the mother, not because the mother is needed for security, but because she is needed to maintain the illusion of perfection, allowing the child to remain his or her ideal.

It is, of course, an illusory closeness. In actuality, a mother shows her attunement with the child by encouraging growth away from her, away from the illusion of perfection. A mother who cooperates with the child in maintaining the illusion is out of touch with the child's actual needs, even if her actions seem to be in the interest of closeness. Therefore a mother's healthy endorsement of her child's burgeoning autonomy reflects an actual closeness or attunement that leads away from illusory closeness. Due to their attunement with the child's needs, most mothers welcome their child's burgeoning competence. Even when autonomy takes an unpleasant form, such as struggles over toilet training, mothers and other caretakers normally accept the situation and applaud the child's progress and growth. This may be bittersweet for the child, whose ambivalence about becoming separate is not entirely matched in the mother.

The vehicle for pulling away from the mother and beginning to develop the competencies the mother will applaud is self-assertion, or the child's own drives toward independence and autonomy. If the child is to stay with the illusion of mother–infant perfection, self-assertion must be refused or disguised. The lust for mastery and autonomy is, in effect, a ticket on a trip that leads away from the mother of physical contact and away therefore from being one's own ideal. There are in fact a variety of ways the adolescent seeking to preserve union with the mother of physical contact can negate self-assertion, and one way to understand the different types of resistance shown by out-of-control adolescents is to see each as a means of allowing the youth to avoid assertiveness or at least avoid the psychological separateness that comes with it. The masochistic patient, for instance, insists through weakness and passivity that he or she has no separate will or intention apart from the mother. The narcissistic adolescent, for another example, demands that the world be a place that is in agreement or conformity with his or her wishes. This negates the effect of self-assertion; if the world is one with my wishes, I do not need to assert anything. Similarly, the mistrustful adolescent avoids the experience of willfulness through perpetual conflict with others. Such an individual never takes the initiative or acts; he or she is forever *re*acting to others.

The adolescent using the schizoid defense has a slightly different problem with self-assertion than do other out-of-control youths. With other types of resistance (or other types of narcissistic disturbance), it was presumably some sort of closeness with the mother that was disturbed by the child's desire to grow and become competent. The latter was therefore jettisoned in order to preserve the illusions that could be built on that early closeness. This is not, however, the situation faced in early childhood by patients who move in a schizoid direction. Closeness with the mother of physical contact miscarried with these patients, as their primary caretakers were apparently not attuned to them, leaving nothing to push away from. In this case, self-assertion comes to equal aloneness, or the sense that the world is not interested or invested in the child. Oneness with the mother of physical contact is an illusion for such children, something yearned for but not reliably and predictably available. In such a world oneness is manufactured in fantasy by the child, perhaps, but it cannot be leaned on or relied upon, and therefore it cannot be pushed away from and left behind.

Such a child avoids self-assertion because it explodes the needed illusion of closeness with the mother of physical contact. The schizoid defense is a means of avoiding situations in which this would become clear, or situations in which the child would find that there is no oneness to call him or her back from autonomous strivings. Autonomy, initiative, or self-assertion are phenomena that must be developed and played out in the context of regret. Their pursuit must cost the individual something, namely the illusion of oneness. If there is no oneness to leave behind, the child asserts himself or herself in a vacuum; there is no close caretaker to push away. Self-assertion therefore leads to feeling utterly alone. The schizoid defense is in essence to choose aloneness in order to avoid having aloneness forced upon the individual.

TREATMENT APPROACHES

Treatment with youths using the schizoid defense is extremely difficult on an outpatient basis, since these patients' passivity can defeat the therapist's attempts at engagement. The therapist has no good way to become real to the patient in only one or two hours per week, and it is easy for treatment to bog down. Residential treatment is more promising, since intrusion into the patient's aloneness can be more intense and unrelenting. Nonetheless there are techniques that can be used by outpatient therapists as well as those working in a residential setting to try to reach such patients and arouse their interest in some more genuine relationship with the therapist (and with themselves).

In general, treatment approaches fall into three categories: making the therapist real to the patient, making the patient's body real to the patient, and helping the patient experience strong affect. Each type of intervention is an attempt to defeat the patient's passivity and disengagement and to force, at least momentarily, interactions and experiences in which both self and other seem more alive and authentic. Each type of intervention will be discussed in turn.

Making the Therapist Real

It is hard to impact a patient who experiences almost everyone, including the therapist, as emotionally thin and arid or, at best, as having the same emotional significance as a character on a television show. The adolescent using the schizoid defense is trying to make sure the therapist does not matter emotionally, that no need of the therapist is experienced. The patient is not trying to interact with the therapist, or with anyone else for that matter. He or she is willing to go through the motions, but does not seek a genuine encounter with the therapist. There is always a distance between patient and therapist that buffers the patient. The therapist must find ways to *intrude* into the isolation the patient has established.

Intrusion may be accomplished through manipulating the physical distance between the patient and therapist, either increasing or decreasing the distance. Therapists cannot simply talk about the patient's detachment; their goal must be to make the patient experience the distance. Only as the patient feels the distance (or closeness) can the therapist talk about it in ways that will be real to the patient. The physical distance must become a sustained metaphor for the patient's private experience of other people.

Therapists may move their chairs closer to the patient. This should be done without comment, either moving a little closer every few minutes or, perhaps, moving very close all at once. The patient is likely to comment on this and ask why the therapist is moving. The therapist should not answer the question but should instead ask about the patient's experience of the situation. Therapists may ask, for instance, whether the distance really matters to the patient or whether the patient likes it better one way or the other. Therapists may also ask whether it is easier or harder to talk when they are close at hand. Therapists should make comments on their perception of the patient, noting the ways the patient seems different and commenting too on how the therapist's experience of the patient changes.

The patient will probably be uncomfortable as the therapist moves closer. If the therapist is within a foot or two the patient is likely to be very uneasy. However, the therapist should not necessarily move back. Whether the therapist stays or retreats should depend on how anxious (or angry) the patient is. It is not a good idea to move back unless the patient clearly cannot tolerate it. Certainly the therapist ought not back off simply because the patient is anxious or tense. The tension is therapeutic, since it indicates that the therapist has had an impact. There is no reason to diminish the distance unless the patient appears unable to bear it. If the therapist decides to move back, the patient may be asked to decide how much or even asked to move the therapist's chair where the patient wants it to be.

As a therapist moves toward a patient, a laboratory of sorts is created, one in which the patient's reactions are material for analysis or comment. Therapists can ask the patient, for instance, if other people always bother the patient as much as the therapist seems to be doing or whether the patient also has trouble with other kinds of closeness. The goal is to look for some way to make the patient interested in his or her response to the therapist.

One patient had been telling the therapist that he did not know how involved in therapy he wished to be, that he had never had any relationship work well for him. At the start of his eighth session he announced he had decided that other people were too painful to bother with and that he did not want any more to do with the therapist. He said that he planned to be silent for the rest of the session and for any future sessions he was forced to attend until the therapist gave up. The therapist waited a few minutes to see if he meant what he said, and after five silent minutes decided the patient probably did intend to remain quiet. The therapist picked up his chair and moved to within a foot of the patient, who promptly protested. The therapist replied that he was surprised to hear the patient say anything and asked why he decided to end his silence so soon. The patient said, "You're too close, damnit!" The therapist replied, "Maybe I'm too real." This opened a window for seeing just why the patient wished to withdraw.

Therapists may also move away from the patient, again without comment, either inching away or dramatically moving off. The patient can be expected to ask what is going on, and, as before, therapists should reply obliquely if at all. They may ask the patient whether it matters, for instance, or they can inquire about the patient's experience of the situation. They may also say something enigmatic, such as "I was trying to see if I could get as far away as you." Therapists may in fact leave the room without explaining why, perhaps telling the patient to "keep on working just like you would if I were here" or saying nothing at all. If the patient protests or asks for an explanation therapists may act surprised and say that they did not know it mattered. They may then demand to know why it matters.

Finally, the patient may be asked to move out of the therapist's sight. For instance the patient may be asked to turn his or her chair around so that the therapist cannot be seen, or the patient may be asked to sit behind a plant or piece of furniture. Therapists should then wait to hear what the patient makes of the situation, hoping the patient is uneasy or ill at ease. Even though the patient is moving physically away from the therapist, this is nonetheless an intrusion; it is so unusual that the patient cannot ignore what is happening and is called out of his or her detachment.

When these sorts of interventions are used, therapists are trying to create a situation in which the patient will need something from them—either release from the discomfort the patient feels or at the very least some explanation of what is going on. If this occurs, the patient has been stymied in the attempt not to need the therapist and to reduce the therapist to the status of an inanimate object.

One late adolescent was shy and passive. He said little in sessions beyond how uneasy he was and that he did not know what to say. He said it bothered him that the therapist sat and looked at him, and he wished the therapist would talk instead of him. The therapist then asked the patient to move out of his line of sight, behind a large chair. The patient was not happy about the idea but complied and spent the rest of that session and the next three appointments completely out of sight. At first he could only talk of how odd the situation was, but he then began to talk about how uneasy he had always been with other people, how much he wished he could be invisible. A period of work and real change followed, lasting several months.

I am aware that all of this has a certain gamelike feel to it. However, I believe that the only way to communicate with someone who is detached and isolated is indirectly, by arranging an experience or encounter that makes the patient wrestle with his or her detachment. Certainly words do not cross the gulf the patient has created. Therapists are trying in the only way left to them to call the patient's attention to the fact they (the therapists) are real, to create an exchange that shakes the patient's lack of relatedness by intruding into it.

Making the Patient's Body Real

Disembodiment is the single trait shared by adolescents using the schizoid defense and also by those suffering schizoid pathology. It is part of the core of a schizoid experience of the world. Certainly no sense of engagement or aliveness is possible without some sense of being one's physical self. A successful treatment is not likely without some attempt at engaging this issue.

The task is to make the patient experience his or her body. Again, words will not suffice; talking *about* one's body is itself detached— the simple act of putting something into words is already one step away from immediate experience. The patient must be placed in a position in which the body asserts itself. The physical body is, after all, compelling for most persons. The therapeutic task is to help the patient's body regain some of its compelling quality.

Therapists must not, however, do or say anything that is likely to be experienced by the patient as sexual in nature. In my experience many out-of-control adolescents—those using the schizoid defense included—have been sexually used during childhood by adults. These patients already have the idea that adults may be exploitative and the associated idea that the body is a source of vulnerability, something that attracts predators. The danger is no less if the therapist is of the same sex as the patient. Such patients will be no less sensitive to the possibility of a homosexual encounter than to a heterosexual one.

Whatever therapists do to help the patient experience the body as real must be asexual.

One possible strategy is to arrange for physical exercise. The logistics of such an approach may be difficult and indeed impossible during some seasons of the year, and vigorous physical activity may be impossible for some therapists and patients. If possible, however, therapists may arrange to spend sessions jogging with the patient, taking a brisk hike, or playing basketball. In fact any situation that allows for a strenuous activity will serve. The goal is to make the patient exercise vigorously enough to feel it. A racing, pounding heart, burning muscles, gasping lungs, and perspiration are hard to ignore. These experiences make the body real, at least briefly, whether the patient wishes it or not.

During or just after vigorous activity is a good time to raise important issues. A patient who is physically alive, even briefly, may be less able to remain indifferent and detached from the important people and events in his or her life. It is not likely that the patient will arrive at a key insight or have some sort of breakthrough experience; nothing so dramatic is probable. However, there is value in bringing these patients to talk of their lives at a time when their defenses are lowered. It may be harder for patients to make others unreal when the body seems more real, or harder to detach from life and its problems when the body feels alive.

> One late adolescent was very heavily involved with drugs and alcohol, had dropped out of school, and led a solitary life. When his parents brought him for treatment he was spending most of his time in his room and had only one friend, whom he seldom saw. He did not date, take part in any group activity, or even talk with others on the phone. He was essentially closed off from contact with others. In sessions he was vague and unfocused. He could not speak two complete sentences about any important subject in his life. His only passion seemed to be food; he was putting on weight, which drew criticism from his family, although he seemed unconcerned. His therapist began having sessions at a nearby jogging trail, where he and the patient would jog while they talked. This was very hard for

the patient, who was badly out of shape, and it did not take much activity before he was out of breath and in need of a rest. The therapist found that the patient was less detached under such circumstances than while sitting in the therapist's office.

Therapists who are unable to use vigorous activity to bring the patient's body to life might use just the opposite approach, relaxation techniques. While deep relaxation techniques are usually thought of in relation to anxiety disorders, their effect is to produce a rather intense experience of the body. A patient may be less able to be abstracted and unreal at a time when the body is in the forefront of awareness.

In residential or even day treatment settings, other interactions may be possible that make the patient's body figural. Staff may help a disembodied patient with hygiene, or they may assign some task that both requires vigorous physical activity and allows others to appreciate what the patient has done. The goal of such interventions is to imply to the patient that the body may be a means of making pleasurable contact with others.

After evening showers, the staff at a residential center took care to brush a female patient's hair and help her style it. This affectionate exchange came to mean a lot to the patient, whose hygiene had been quite poor and whose general manner had been to wander around the unit in a physically awkward, robotic way.

One young man maintained a withdrawn, aloof manner no matter what the activity. Even while playing vigorous sports he kept an utterly blank expression on his face, so that it was impossible to know what impacted him in any way. He was helped to draw an outline of his body on a large roll of paper and then was asked to add his body parts and features, telling what he liked and disliked about each one. At first he was unmoved and indifferent as he worked, but as the project continued he became increasingly agitated and began to protest that he did not see the point. While no new or important content came from any of this, staff noticed that at the project's conclusion he was for the first time showing facial expressions when he played sports with his peers and also when he told jokes.

A female patient was hard to reach. She was always very much alone, even when she was with others. Staff sought to make emotional contact through friendly physical contact. They patted her shoulder as they talked to her or lightly touched her arm as they greeted her. When she was called on to talk in group therapy, they often held her hand, asking what that was like for her and whether the experience prompted any memories or feelings. After two weeks of this the patient was much more lively and interactive, and staff were able to engage the patient without making physical contact.

Helping the Patient Experience Strong Affect

Most exchanges in therapy are verbal and fairly descriptive in nature. The majority of patients bring emotionally charged issues to sessions, and the therapist does not need to do anything to encourage affect. Needless to say, matters are quite different with patients using the schizoid defense. Lively affect is not welcome to patients trying to keep the inner world asleep and nonproblematic. Therapists may find sessions so affectively vacant that they become bored or sleepy.

Patients using the schizoid defense often talk in a stiff, unproductive way. Their language is empty, so that the therapist is not sure what, if anything, can be responded to. Patients may speak of matters that sound important, but these subjects never go anywhere. The patient is staying on the surface, talking emptily or abstractly, but not *really*. Superficial, stilted, and empty language protects patients from the anxiety they would feel if the inner world started to come to life. This language also mediates the patient's interaction with the world, keeping the world and the patient safely apart.

What this sort of language reveals is an impoverished affective experience, that these patients have little range and depth to what they feel. Such patients need to develop many more varieties of affective experience, beginning to enrich their limited range of emotion and stir thereby an interest in the world. This does not mean, however, that therapists should try to teach patients new words that would allow them to distinguish a wider range of feelings, for instance, that there is a difference between being pleased and being elated or between being irritated and being angry. Patients who rely on the schizoid defense will tune out this sort of instruction; even if they comply and learn new words, the words will be used mechanically, merely to get the therapist to back off. Nothing will be accomplished by trying to expand the patient's affective language.

Patients may, however, learn something about a broader range of affect by seeing their therapists be affectively alive in sessions. It is up to therapists to bring emotion into sessions through their words and through what might be termed their style of behavior. Therapists should, for instance, use words that refer to the body and bodily functions, and they should feel comfortable using terms that have some shock value, such as "dirty" words and phrases. Any phrase that might shock the patient or evoke some feeling is useful. Therapists should also consider using what might be called adolescent humor, or humor built around sexual anxieties (if this can be done without being sexually provocative). The idea is to use a more evocative language than is usual in therapy sessions. Such a language makes an impact on the other person and demonstrates that the therapist is comfortable with the other person's feelings.

Therapists should also behave in sessions with what might be called controlled spontaneity (Cohen and Sherwood 1991). They may raise and lower their voice dramatically, for instance, as they speak, in a deliberate effort to increase and decrease their impact. They may also make sudden movements, lurching forward in their chairs or even springing to their feet as they make some point. Therapists may also do such things as clap their hands together for emphasis or slap the arm of their chair when they make a point. These and other dramatic gestures tend to slip under the patient's passivity and make some impact by showing emotional aliveness and bringing about some emotional arousal in the patient.

A therapist went out of his way to be affectively warm with one late adolescent schizoid patient. He always smiled warmly when he greeted the patient and shook his hand, usually holding the patient's hand for a moment with both of his. Similarly the therapist took pains to be more energetic (and less abstract) in responding to what the patient said. After a few sessions the patient began to show more facial expressions during sessions, losing to some degree the masklike face that had previously been typical.

A late adolescent patient was passive, uninvolved, and withdrawn, both in sessions and out. In an effort to have an impact on him, the therapist tended to use evocative language, especially language related to bodily functions. The first time the therapist drew any spontaneous reaction from the patient occurred after the patient said, in a mechanical way, that he saw little of his father since his parents divorced; the patient said he thought his father's new wife did not want him to see any of his old family very much. The therapist asked the patient if he had seen his father naked recently. The patient was (understandably) shocked at the question and asked what the therapist meant. The therapist replied that it sounded as if the new wife had "cut off your dad's dick and put it some place for safekeeping—if we could find out where she's hidden it, we could give it back to him and he could make his own decisions." This deliberately chosen oedipal level imagery made the patient anxious, and he laughed and came to life. He was then able to speak briefly of his impression that women are stronger than men and control them.

Finally, therapists may try to bring patients to life affectively by making them more aware of their inner worlds. Patients may become enlivened through attending to their dreams. The therapist might focus for a time entirely on dream material, for instance, or the patient might be required to keep a journal of dreams. The idea behind this strategy is that the patient's contact with primary process material is likely to produce some affective motility. Of course, patients using the schizoid defense are almost certain to say they cannot recall any dreams. In this case therapists may say that they dreamed about the patient the night before the session. Therapists may then manufacture a dream, preferably one containing themes that might reasonably be expected to be of significance to the patient.

The use of dream material—real or manufactured—is intended to be regressive, to make patients slide back into emotions they would rather ignore or suppress, to bring them to life affectively. A final technique to use in achieving this aim is placing the patient in the analytic position, that is, having the patient lie down on a couch, while the therapist sits out of sight, saying little. Patients who can see the therapist face to face should have an easier time hanging onto detachment and indifference. Patients who cannot see the therapist and who are in an unstructured, ill-defined situation ("Just say whatever comes to mind") may be less able to defend themselves against emotional aliveness and may also feel more need of the therapist. The analytic position is simply more likely to produce regression than a face-to-face position, and this is its value with adolescents using the schizoid defense.

CASE EXAMPLE

It may be helpful now to offer an example of an out-of-control adolescent using the schizoid defense. The patient to be described, David, was treated for ten months at a residential treatment center. At the time of admission David was nearly 17 years of age, and it was clear that his problems had been building for many years. David's parents, both of whom were successful attorneys, were divorced, and each had remarried. David lived with his father in New York, while his mother and two stepbrothers lived in Florida. David had actually spent most of his growing-up years with his mother but had moved to his father's home after his problems became too much for his mother to handle. He was brought to residential treatment after he became too obviously disturbed for his father and stepmother to deal with, and after the stepmother came to feel that David might even pose a threat to her and David's father's young son.

It is not easy to characterize the problems that David showed just before admission. It appeared that he had been gradually withdrawing from reality into something of a fantasy-driven private world. He had trouble concentrating on courses at school, withdrew almost entirely from his peers, began using drugs, and became unresponsive to parental rules and wishes. The latter led to monumental battles with his father and stepmother, and on one occasion David reportedly threatened to harm his younger stepbrother. David then started to run away from home. During the last such event he stole a car and the driver's wallet and embarked on a cross-country trip during which he imagined he was a crime boss who was recruiting new members for his gang. During this trip, which moved from New York to Utah, David behaved much as a spy might: he frequently hid by day and crept up to homes and businesses by night, carefully stealing what-ever he needed at the time. In Utah he suddenly came to his senses and called his father, who arranged for his return home. He then had two brief hospitalizations in New York, which were unsuccessful, before being admitted to reconstructive residential treatment.

Those working with David initially misunderstood the case, which shows some of the diagnostic difficulties with adolescent patients. David's cross-country crime spree was known, but the fact that he had been living in a fantasy for its duration was not. He was therefore approached as someone moving in an antisocial direction. It was easy to make such a mistake, since David had almost no ability to articu-late his inner world or talk about himself. In response to questions the staff learned that he felt no particular guilt or regret for what he had done, and he did not seem to have any warm feelings for his family or anyone else. He came across as a somewhat indulged and perhaps entitled child of rich parents, lacking empathy and conscience—hence the initial wrong diagnostic formulation.

Only with time did those working with David learn to what ex-tent he was living on the edge of reality and how disengaged he was from the world of others. People did not seem entirely real to him, nor were his own actions fully real. His lack of remorse stemmed from the fact that he did not feel that *he* had actually done anything. The events of his life were things that just happened, not the result of his own volition. This left David in a quasi-substantial, somewhat dream-like world. It was only after some time that those working with David realized how alienated and alone he was.

In David's case the schizoid defense was his means of avoiding intrusions by an angry and chaotic mother, intrusions that David's father did nothing to protect him from—indeed, David's father was in his own way quite intrusive. Both parents, though especially the mother, had managed to convey that they wanted David to feel whatever they felt, and neither parent had any tolerance for David's own feelings when these proved different. Neither parent was attuned to David, and both imposed their own emotions and needs onto their son, accepting him if he absorbed their emotions (usually anger) but rejecting him if he failed to match their moods and feelings. This meant that David could be connected with his parents only if he had no autonomous strivings; independence, however, came at the cost of aloneness. In order to preserve some fragment of himself, David chose a different sort of aloneness, one into which his parents could not intrude. He hid himself for protection.

When treatment began to focus on David's alienation from the social world, he did not respond positively. This approach asked David to endure much more intimate contact with other people than he preferred, and he looked more disorganized and confused. However, as he grew more disorganized, he also started to tell his staff and peers of the psychotic fantasy he had lived in during his cross-country trip. The treatment center's staff came to see this fantasy as David's attempt to be both powerful and a hero, which was probably age-appropriate for a middle adolescent male, although in David's case this age-appropriate aim had taken a grotesque turn.

Sessions between David and his mother gave clues to the origins of David's problems. One of the mother's close relatives grew terminally ill, and she was understandably distressed. In sessions, however, the mother did not keep her distress as her own but seemed to be trying to give it away to David. She rebuked him for not loving the sick relative as much as she did and was fairly open in trying to induce guilt and upset. The mother was intensely angry, volatile, and actually quite destructive whenever she was distressed and had a way of making everyone else feel as chaotic as she felt. After much work, most of it related to the sick relative, David began to learn to keep a healthy distance from his mother's feelings, acknowledging them but not necessarily sharing them. After five weeks of hard work on this subject, David tacitly declared his emotional independence from the mother by saying that he did not feel as she did on some topic. The mother became enraged, then despondent, and finally broke off all contact for several months following this session.

When his mother withdrew, David suddenly began to feel strong desires to elope from the treatment center and told this to his staff and peers. It appeared to staff that David wanted to run to his mother and effect some reconciliation with her, although he did not consciously wish to do this. The problem for David was how to preserve his growing desire to be a separate person from his mother and yet withstand the aloneness he felt when his mother retaliated for this desire. David needed over a month to master his urges to elope, but when he did master them, he was more alive and confident than he had ever been.

David then began to articulate feelings of inadequacy. He seemed to feel inadequate in every way that an adolescent could. He was certain there was not enough to him to satisfy another person and that he would surely be rejected if he tried to make contact with people. Consequently he had adopted a mechanical, robotic manner with others that both insulated him and also evoked the rejection he feared from others. With time and effort, David risked being more spontaneous with those around him and gradually became less wooden and more genuine.

By the time of discharge David was fairly comfortable in the social world and was in fact popular with his peers. He had become interested in running and had entered several long distance races in which he had done well; this had given him a sense of being physically alive that was new to him. David was still very uneasy with sexuality and did not appear ready to date. He had, however, become competent in dealing with his mother, keeping his distance from her and yet making himself available for a limited relationship. He was not able to establish a reliable relationship with his father, who late in treatment had become angry that David was not sure he wanted to live at the father's home. However, David was able to accept the way things were with his father, largely because he had the newfound ability to make friends and draw on those relationships for companionship and affection. Nearly one year after discharge he was doing well. David was attending college, had maintained abstinence from drugs, and had friends with whom he regularly spent time.

CHAPTER 8

THE AFFECTIVELY LABILE ADOLESCENT

THE UNDERLYING PICTURE

It is probably not possible to identify the affectively labile adolescent on the basis of presenting symptoms or on the basis of the patient's interpersonal style with the therapist. There is a very wide range of problems that might bring these patients to treatment and an equally wide range of styles in the therapy session. Some of these patients will seem hostile and defiant, others masochistic, still others passive and affiliative, and some will even vary across sessions. In order to identify patients using affective lability as a form of resistance, the therapist will have to look at underlying characteristics, at patterns, motives, and traits that are implied by what the patient says and does. With time, the following underlying characteristics emerge.

The most obvious feature of the psychological landscape is mood instability. Affectively labile patients are particularly prone to depression, and in particular to depression that has an angry and desperate quality. These patients find their moods to be a mystery. Their experience is that moods swing dramatically without warning or obvious cause and without their control. Consequently, they may feel themselves sliding suddenly into a dark and painful state with no sense of what they can do to understand or manage the situation. These patients feel as if the mood were entirely alien or external to themselves, something that comes upon them from the outside. The result is that they live in anxiety over the next sea change in their feelings. Each mood swing threatens to cast them into a deep distress they can (as they see it) do nothing about.

When moods are experienced as alien, affects are experienced in their extreme forms. We are able to modulate affect by learning that even the most painful feelings do not last forever and that other persons will stay connected with us when we are in distress. These discoveries—usually made by the growing child over years—allow us to experience moods as *ours*, as a familiar part of our world and who we are. In turn, when moods feel predictable and familiar, the sense of panic that may otherwise accompany painful affect is removed. The absence of panic allows the child to discover that it is the nature of feelings to change and that they can therefore be endured. In such a psychological atmosphere the child has the opportunity to distinguish among gradations of emotion—learning, for instance, that sadness is different from despair or that liking someone is not the same as adoring them.

If, however, the child has not been able to learn that feelings change or has found that painful affect tends to open a gulf with other people, then emotion remains an urgent matter, a crisis. For such a person, painful affect is not something that can be endured but is something to be gotten away from as fast as possible. In this atmosphere the child cannot learn to moderate strong affect, and feelings remain extreme. Such an individual experiences panic when others would feel worry, rage when others would be irritated, and despair when others would be merely upset. Feelings are always intense and barely manageable, and the child lacks the leisure to discover a broader, less intense range of affect.

These two traits—unstable mood and affect that moves toward the extreme—are closely joined with a third characteristic, a distorted time sense. I have already referred to the sense of urgency that attends these patients' experience of strong emotion. They can feel such urgency because their sense of time tends too much toward what is momentary. They do not experience time in a sufficiently broad context but focus too much on the present instant, tending to feel that whatever they experience now will go on forever. Indeed, such patients may say they know intellectually their feelings will change but that they nonetheless cannot shake the sense that they will never feel differently than they now do.

When time is only *this moment*, affect is necessarily exaggerated. The hallmark of this sort of time distortion is that it turns every experience into a matter of urgency or crisis. Pleasant feelings are intensified and move toward euphoria or elation, while painful feelings become unbearable. Liking someone on a date can turn into intoxication with that person, while the sadness of breaking up with a boyfriend or girlfriend can become a nearly suicidal despair. Without a sense of time as something that moves continuously, it is hard to appreciate the way feelings can ebb and flow, and yet this appreciation is what makes feelings manageable.

If time perspectives are lost, the concept of waiting must also be lost. Waiting is only something that can be endured if we experience the passage of time as relatively benign. Waiting otherwise amounts to losing something that was within our grasp or of being subjected to unending and unchanging torture. Indeed, a number of important personal and interpersonal competencies are built on the ability to wait, which is essentially the ability to put matters into context instead of reacting to every event as if it had monumental importance. The most important of these competencies includes the capacity to put a distressing event into the background and carry on with what else has to be done, eventually returning to the painful event when more pressing matters have been taken care of. A second and related competency might be termed the fine art of not overreacting. It is typical of impulsive and immature individuals that they react to any particular event as if that single episode took place in a vacuum and were the only thing of importance; waiting allows the individual to learn what else, if anything, is relevant and therefore to react to the entire event rather than simply a fragment.

A fourth characteristic of affectively labile adolescents is their intolerance of pain. Pain cannot be endured when it is experienced as something that is inflicted from the outside and lasts indefinitely. In order to bear emotional pain, we must have confidence that it is time-limited and that it makes some sense in the context of what is happening in our lives. With these confidences we feel durable, that our selves and our world can continue. Otherwise, emotional pain threatens to sweep the self away, as though we had lost the familiar "me" and any world in which we might belong or be at home. Pain therefore becomes something to be gotten rid of in any way possible, either through reckless behaviors that offer tension relief and distraction, drugs that induce an alternate state of mind, or activities that, in effect, ask others to take care of us.

It is not possible to adapt to life without being able to tolerate emotional pain. Without this ability, the individual is tense and fearful. The world cannot be trusted if at any minute one's feelings can turn dramatically and traumatically negative. It is impossible to relax or to drop one's guard under such circumstances; life becomes a matter of watching for any sign that an emotional crisis is about to break and desperately trying to avoid or defuse it. Consequently, nothing can be approached with hope or confidence, and life feels like a long journey on thin ice.

The four underlying characteristics of affectively labile adolescents, then, are: unstable mood, extreme forms of affect, a sense of time dominated by urgency, and intolerance of painful affect. Those working with these patients will not, in all likelihood, be able to see these four characteristics in the first sessions. For one thing, these are underlying traits, as opposed to manifest symptoms, and so they have to be deduced from the patient's words and behavior. Beyond that, however, the last trait, intolerance of pain, means that these patients try to stay utterly unaware of "where it hurts." Generally they do not try to reflect on their problems or articulate them to others, since even the briefest recollection of a problem can trigger an episode of depression and anxiety. These patients are unlikely to tell the therapist very much that would expose them to such distress.

We should remember that these patients behave in out of control ways precisely to avoid such distress. Their drug use is plainly aimed at eliminating painful states of mind or inducing a sense of euphoria. Their propensity for conflict with parents and other authority figures is at least in part a means of making a personal problem into an interpersonal one, or of "giving" some of their pain to those around them. Similarly, whatever wild behaviors they show are attempts at discharging painful affect through behaviors that are distracting, exciting, and offer the opportunity artificially to raise and then relieve the tension level. An individual with so many means of relieving distress will not feel a deep need for a therapist. Such adolescents are, therefore, not likely to reveal themselves in early sessions in ways that would allow the therapist to see clearly their underlying characteristics.

THE USE OF OTHER PEOPLE TO MANAGE PAIN

Affectively labile adolescents do not like to be alone. Some such adolescents cannot stand being physically alone; they feel uneasy by themselves, as if menaced in some vague way. Even those who can tolerate physical aloneness for periods of time do so only if they feel connected to another person. These are needy and dependent individuals who cling to others desperately. If a relationship ends, they tend to replace the lost love object very quickly. They must: the other person is their buffer against pain.

The problem for the affectively labile adolescent is not so much other people as the self. These patients have a hard time being with themselves. They do not experience themselves as ongoing centers of autonomy and initiative but as flimsy vessels who can be swamped by any emotional wave. They are intensely uneasy with themselves and are driven to attach to someone else in whose shadow they might live, hoping to get away from the risks that go with being separate and independent. Consequently, they seek other persons to whom they may belong. If their attention is fixed on the other person and on the close union they feel with that person, they may forget themselves, which is what they want.

This pattern of relationships has been explored in the psychoanalytic literature. Among others, Burgner and Edgcumbe (1972) and Anna Freud (1952, 1965) outlined attachments based on need of the other person, as opposed to the capacity to be attached even when the other person is not needed for any particular task or function. When relationships are built on need, rather than on a constant attachment, the other person's *function* is valued more than the other as a person. In the case of the affectively labile patient, the other is asked to fill the function of defining the patient, of keeping the patient company in such a way that the patient is relieved of being on his or her own.

Affectively labile patients are anxious and depressed when alone and forced to live on their own, and there is relief at being embedded in another person. This embeddedness and attendant tension relief is the function the loved one is asked to play in the patient's psychic economy. However, since it is the function that is important—not the person—people tend to be interchangeable. At least to some extent, anyone able to offer this sort of tension relief and embeddedness will do. Affectively labile patients can therefore replace a lost love object quickly; they do not need to grieve the loss of the other person, since they did not lose the person but the person's tension-reducing function.

It is a small step from believing that relationships are built on need to believing that they are built on neediness. This is the case with affectively labile patients, who feel that relationships require one person to be strong and the other to be needy. Needless to say, this does not lead to mature or stable attachments. There is little sense that there can be mutuality in relationships, that relationships consist of two equal mutually contributing partners who care for one another consistently. Rather, these patients believe that relationships endure only so long as one person desperately needs the other. When the other person meets the patient's needs, there may be a sense of satisfaction bordering on elation. The patient feels a closeness that approaches fusion, as the patient feels that the other person truly cares.

The problem with such relationships is that they are so unstable. For one thing, as soon as a need has been met, and the resulting euphoria is experienced, matters are again uncertain. Since the patient believes that relationships are built on need, there is the danger of not needing the other enough and the attendant danger that the other will then lose interest. Thus, as soon as one need is met, another must be found. Those who have worked with these adolescents are familiar with the pattern: there seems always to be some crisis, usually a silly one, with the patient almost constantly turning to a friend or lover for help or support in a matter that seems desperate to the patient but trivial to an outsider.

One variation on the theme is that the patient will often cause a crisis in the relationship. The patient may be seen to pick a fight over something utterly senseless with the apparent intent of simply raising the tension level. In fact, this is precisely what the patient is trying to do. At some point in this self-inflicted crisis, the patient will give in and try to effect a reconciliation. If the effort is successful, the patient will feel closer to the other person than before the crisis. The sequence is not unlike that of a baby who becomes hungry, fusses and cries, then has a good feed, and settles back into satiation. Similarly, the patient causes a rift and raises (both personal and interpersonal) tension until it is felt to be unbearable. Then the patient submits to the other person and feels intense satisfaction. The whole sequence is a means of being reassured of the other's love. Since love is felt to be based on need and the meeting of needs, the patient must have frequent crises through which the other can be seen as devoted and caring.

Such a relationship wears out the other person. Even if the other begins the relationship with good will and sincere feelings, the constant crises and the sense that the patient is demanding much and contributing little erodes interest. Often the other person does not begin the relationship with sincere interest; sadistic and opportunistic individuals are attracted to affectively labile individuals, who are easy to take advantage of. Affectively labile adolescents are often roughed up or beaten by those they date; they are also frequent victims of date rape, and those they date frequently cheat on them. These sadistic behaviors would end relationships with healthier people, of course. However, they may simply cause a crisis for the affectively labile person who eventually submits, reconciles, and feels "everything is okay now, and he (or she) will never do that again."

Another and perhaps more important problem with relationships built on neediness is that the patient cannot afford to become stronger or more mature. These are essentially the dynamics we see in adult borderline cases (Cohen and Sherwood 1991, Kroll 1988). If the patient feels that others will care only as long as they are desperately needed, then the patient must stay desperately needy. Competence and maturity come at a huge risk, namely aloneness. The patient fears that any competence on his or her part would lead the other person to feel no longer needed. The other might then leave, feeling (as the patient supposes) that the patient can now take care of him- or herself.

Once such patients are in treatment, they cannot afford to make progress. If they take any significant steps forward, they fear that others will see their gains, feel the patient no longer needs them, and end the relationship. Any progress must therefore be undone. It is a common sight to see such patients make good use of treatment only at some point to lose quickly and dramatically all they have done. They are, of course, trying to reassure others that they are no stronger than they were and that they remain as much in need of the other person as they ever were.

If neediness is the means to maintaining a relationship, it is also the means for repairing it. Since relationships built on neediness tend to be unstable, affectively labile adolescents find themselves threatened with loss of a needed other fairly frequently. This is an intolerable situation for these patients, who genuinely feel unable to carry on alone and are therefore desperate to get the other person back. These patients must therefore communicate to the other person that they have no self or life apart from the relationship. They do this by falling apart emotionally when faced with the other person's desire to end matters. It is not at all unusual for such patients to threaten suicide or make some suicidal gesture in this situation. The message to the other person is, "You can't leave—it will cost my sanity or even my life." Affectively labile patients are willing to degrade themselves and jettison all pretense to pride in order to renew the endangered relationship, promising whatever seems necessary and showing levels of neediness that would be embarrassing to most adolescents.

Most suicidal gestures and instances of self-mutilation in this patient group occur in the context of a broken relationship. I do not believe that these patients want to die or hurt themselves at these times, although they may indeed kill themselves or inflict serious injuries accidentally. Their intent is much as it was throughout the relationship, to parade themselves as persons in great need who cannot adapt or live without the other to lean on. It is a way of assuring the other that they still have the basis on which the relationship was built—their weakness—and that they can be even more weak if that is necessary.

As mentioned earlier, these patients can be and are taken advantage of in relationships. They have little sense of their rights and certainly do not see themselves as equal to their partners. It is sad to see the way in which they can so easily be treated badly by others and yet strive to maintain the relationship. They are doomed to this situation, however, by the way they use others to ward off painful affect. No matter what the other person may do to them, being alone seems worse. They are extremely uneasy with anything that hints at emotional separateness.

Those working with these patients may notice that they are typically allergic to conflict and tension with peers, except for the manufactured crises described earlier. Affectively labile patients seek to embed themselves in the other person; they are never quite separate from the other, nor do they seek to be. Consequently, any interaction that implies being a separate person is not welcome. Tension with others implies distance and the capacity to feel *differently*. This hint of being different undermines the fantasy of oneness, and these patients will generally give in rather than behave in any way that perpetuates the tension.

Affectively labile adolescents are usually much better able to tolerate conflict with the adults in their lives, chiefly their parents. At first glance it may seem that this means they feel more confident of these relationships; however, I believe that conflict is one means by which they express closeness with the adults in their lives. These patients are generally tangled up emotionally with their parents as much as with the peers with whom they are close. They show this emotional embeddedness by the fact that they cannot be detached from their parents. They react badly or take offense to exchanges with parents that certainly do not call for such a response, and an outside observer would say they are overreacting. This means that they are taking matters far too *personally*, that there is too little distance between themselves and their parents. The offense they take at their parents and the resulting conflict is the consequence of not feeling separate, of not being able to regard the situation from an appropriate emotional distance. Therefore, they can engage in conflict with their parents and perhaps other adults because the conflict itself is an indication of belonging and closeness, an indication that these adolescents are not yet separate enough to avoid taking matters much too personally. The same situation that makes these patients allergic to conflict with peers they need makes conflict inevitable with their parents.

Affectively labile adolescents are possessive and jealous individuals. This is hardly surprising, since they need the other person so much and are so uneasy with any indication of separateness from the other. If a boyfriend, girlfriend, or best friend shows any particular interest—however innocent—in another person, these patients are likely to be afraid that the relationship is about to end, that the loved one is losing interest and will soon exchange them for the new person. Very often this situation is the occasion for creating a crisis of some sort in order to experience reconciliation and reunion; affectively labile patients may also do something to demonstrate weakness and need in this situation. They are looking for an exclusive relationship, after all; being able to share the other would imply much more separateness than they want to feel.

A 16-year-old girl was shopping at a mall with her boyfriend and best friend. At one point in the trip, her boyfriend and girl friend said a few words to each other off to the side about a store they were about to enter. The patient immediately felt that neither one of them cared for her any longer and that they wanted to be rid of her. Without warning, she suddenly began to sob, which she continued for almost thirty minutes while both tried to comfort her. This was a girl who gravitated toward one or two very close, possessive relationships at a time. Dating relationships seldom lasted more than one or two months, and she tended to wear out her friends only a little less quickly. She had taken an overdose of over-the-counter pain medication one year earlier while feeling that "no one really loved me." She had several times broken framed pictures, grabbed a shard of glass, and made superficial cuts on her arms while in similar states of mind. She was unable to tolerate any interruption in the bond of closeness she sought with those in her life.

Another 16-year-old girl with a history of heavy drug use, running away, and suicide attempts was being treated in a residential facility. The first thing staff noticed about her was that she seemed afraid to make anyone angry. She could not bring herself to confront anyone, even for obviously offensive behavior, and she seemed prepared to absorb any insult in hopes that the other person might eventually like her. Even in group therapy, she only said things that were complimentary to her peers. This behavior paralleled her interactions with peers and those she dated prior to admission. She had been roughed up by numerous boys and date-raped at least once. Her peers also treated her in high-handed ways, but she accepted this, feeling it was the price she would have to pay if anyone were to like her.

A 15-year-old boy with longstanding depressive symptoms and heavy drug use was in residential treatment. Upon moving to a new unit, he formed an almost symbiotic tie with another, low-functioning peer. He could scarcely be separated from the peer without becoming morbid and lethargic. Once the peer became aggressive toward staff and had to be physically restrained. The patient watched with surprise, then looked dazed and confused. Suddenly he fell on the floor in the same position as his friend who was being held down, staying there until staff forced him to get up. He appeared to have entered a dissociative state and had no recollection of the event later.

These patients try to form excessively close relationships in order to manage and keep at bay the painful affect they might otherwise experience. By themselves they feel utterly vulnerable to shifting moods and the pain that entails. With someone to whom they feel close, they can (and try to) forget themselves.

TREATMENT OBSTACLES

Of the different types of resistance shown by out-of-control adolescents, affective lability is the type most likely to persist as a personality style. Affectively labile patients can hardly afford to move emotionally without risking the very moods and extreme affect they were trying to flee. Given how afraid affectively labile adolescents are of painful feelings, any move must feel like a step toward the abyss. On the one hand, these patients can maintain a pattern of relationships based on neediness; this does nothing to solve their problems, but such relationships do distract and insulate them from pain. On the other hand they could take steps toward competence but have to face in the process the very pain that feels so intolerable. The former option may well seem preferable, since competence will appear to these patients as something that leads to being left alone by other people and therefore left alone with an affective life that is volatile and painful. This pattern of resistance can easily become a way of life, and their adolescent resistance may well solidify into adult borderline pathology.

Therapists, however, cannot approach these cases as they would adult borderline patients. Affectively labile adolescents are not able to make use of adult relationships. These patients are not generally able to view adults as potential sources of help and instead almost always turn to peers for the tension-reducing functions they seek from others. This may seem surprising. Since these patients are emotionally unstable and interpersonally needy, it may seem that any port in a storm should do. As a rule, however, these patients cannot see adults as strong and reliable.

One reason for this pattern of chronically impaired relationships with adults is the way in which affectively labile patients deny generational differences. As discussed in Chapter 3, out-of-control adolescents typically deny the difference between adults and children, thereby obliterating the concept of maturity or a gradual progression toward adulthood. Most out-of-control adolescents engage in this denial by seeing themselves as adults already, by overvaluing their own abilities and accomplishments. Affectively labile patients also deny generational differences, but in the reverse manner: they tend to see adults as being as weak and unstable as they are. While most out-of-control adolescents feel they are already the peers of the adults in their lives and therefore need not grow up, affectively labile adolescents see adults as no more capable than they are. There is therefore no place to grow towards. In the affectively labile patient's world, everyone is weak, chaotic, and unreliable.

It is my impression that a disproportionate number of affectively labile patients have been sexually abused as children, and this surely plays a role in the way these patients later see adults. They may be more inclined to view adults as being themselves needy, exploitative, or at least inept if some of the adults in their lives turned to them sexually and if the other adults they knew were unable to protect them from this abuse. Consequently, these patients may well have come to see adults as though they were simply large children. Like other out-of-control patients, they deny generational differences. Unlike other such patients, however, they do this by seeing everyone as childish, no matter what their age.

Those affectively labile adolescents who were not victims of sexual abuse as children may have nonetheless experienced the adults in their lives as childish or weak. It has long been speculated that patients with borderline dynamics come from parents who are themselves suffering borderline pathology. To the extent that this is true, affectively labile patients may have grown up with adults who were not well able to handle the stresses of life and who tended to engage in immature, childish patterns of interaction with others. Over the years, these patients may have formed the impression that adults were more likely to draw emotional supplies from the children of the family than they were to be able to give to the children. The result is the same as with patients who were sexually abused; they view adults as if they were no different from children.

These patients may not be able to articulate their dismal view of adults, but they express this view in their interactions with their parents. They are typically angry and defiant at home, as if they believe that their parents, being weak, have no right to impose limits and restrictions. They often appear to scorn their parents for what weakness they sense there. A variation on this theme occurs when they believe their parents need them emotionally more than they need the parents. In this case they tend to be openly contemptuous of the parent they perceive as being needy. These patients' out-of-control behaviors are, in part, ways of expressing scorn of parental weakness and anger at not being protected from the pain they feel.

When such patients come to therapy, they do not expect much from the therapist. They often imagine that even if the therapist seems steady enough, the truth is otherwise and that at home the therapist behaves as badly as the adults they have known. In short they are prepared to experience the therapist as irrelevant, and are far more willing to seek out a peer for the close relationship that will provide emotional equilibrium.

It is extremely difficult to treat this type of out-of-control adolescent as an outpatient. I believe that residential treatment is far preferable, although it is not, of course, always possible to place patients in such treatment. Outpatient therapists may not even be aware that their patient is affectively labile until after a number of sessions. The patient is not likely to be genuine with the therapist and may completely mask the distress and chaos that characterizes life outside the therapy hour. Therapists may not suspect affective lability until the parents bring disturbing information about self-mutilation or until the patient shows signs of having been roughed up or hit by a sadistic friend or lover. My point is that an outpatient therapist may not even be in position to make a good diagnosis until some crisis breaks. Given the fact that these patients do not readily see adults as sources of help, an outpatient therapist is swimming against the tide.

OUTPATIENT TREATMENT STRATEGIES

If affectively labile patients must be treated as outpatients, sessions should take place twice weekly. It is so hard to find any way into the world these patients inhabit that once-weekly sessions do not leave the therapist with fair chances for having an impact. Unhappily, these patients may well find it difficult to produce enough material to fill two sessions weekly, and they almost certainly cannot fill more than two sessions. Consequently, there is no good reason to attempt three or more sessions.

Therapists should work more closely with families than is the case with most out-of-control adolescents. Given the dismal view of adults held by affectively labile patients, it is important to help the parents become more effective in establishing and enforcing effective limits. Of course, out-of-control youths will have a hard time responding positively to such limits, and matters may well grow worse at home as the parents try. However, this can be positive over the long run. These patients already have the idea that tension cannot be endured. It is important that they see their parents as people who are willing to create and endure the tension caused by limits and the inevitable conflicts these limits cause.

Therapists should make it clear that they are the ones pushing these limits, that they are responsible in large part for the unhappiness at home. Like many out-of-control youths, these patients have probably not had occasion to see adults as willing to cause distress and accept responsibility for it. It may begin to change their view of adults to find that the therapist is different in this respect. If these patients have been sexually used by adults or reared by parents who themselves showed emotional instability, they have not been able to experience adults as committed to growth and maturity, or as willing to take a stand on the side of adult realities. While they will not be happy with the distress the therapist is causing, they may begin to sense that the therapist is committed to a different order of things than they have witnessed at home in the past.

Such an approach will increase the tension level in the therapy hour, which is for the good. Therapy cannot take place unless the patient's symptoms are present in the session, giving the therapist a chance to deal directly with the symptoms. In the case of affectively labile adolescents, handling tension is a core issue. These patients cannot tolerate tension, as outlined earlier, and they typically seek relationships that carry a tension-reducing function. The therapist's strategy is to expose these patients to different responses to tension, demonstrating that tension is not something that must be run from or avoided at all costs and that tension can in fact be endured. On the whole, therapists should not try to make these patients feel better or do anything to lower a patient's tension or distress (an exception will be discussed later).

One possible technique that may serve this aim is the use of the analytic position in the therapy hour (having the patient lie down during sessions) while the therapist sits out of sight. I am not suggesting that therapists should attempt psychoanalysis with these patients but that therapists should avail themselves of the regressive potential inherent in the analytic position. Affectively labile patients will want to avoid the therapist and avoid too having to wrestle with anxiety-producing topics. They tend to stay on the surface of subjects or to talk about what others, usually their parents, have done to them. The analytic position keeps the patient from seeing the therapist's response and, in a sense, leaves the patient alone with his or her thoughts and feelings. It is harder to stay unproductive or on the surface in this situation. It is also harder to avoid regression and, therefore, tension.

> A 16-year-old's parents brought him to therapy after he ran away with a n'er-do-well 22-year-old woman who was already pregnant with someone else's child. The youth insisted there was nothing questionable about the relationship, saying that it was "true love." There was also evidence the patient was involved to some extent with drugs and perhaps antisocial activities as well. However, the patient did not want to discuss any of this but insisted on talking about his parents and how badly they understood him. Finally the therapist placed the patient in the analytic position on the couch, feeling that the patient was far too guarded to say much of importance about himself otherwise. Over the next two sessions the patient gradually became less guarded and controlled. He started to talk about how frightened he felt most of the time and about his sense that everyone else knew how to handle life better than he did—hence his attraction to a woman who was perhaps old enough to "know the ropes." The therapist felt the move had been highly productive, since more important information was now coming out.

The therapist's responses to the patient are probably not as important as what the responses imply. That is, the content of the therapist's interventions does not matter nearly so much as whether those interventions convey comfort with the patient's anxiety. These patients are not likely to be moved or influenced by the content of what the therapist says during the resistance phase of treatment, but they will be influenced by their sense of whether the therapist is uneasy with their discomfort and wishes to decrease it. Therapists must therefore acknowledge and define what the patient feels but should not say anything to make the patient feel better.

This situation tends to make the patient dependent on the therapist to some degree, which is desirable. This is the therapist's chance to introduce the patient to a relationship that is not built on tension reduction, and it may well be the only relationship in the patient's life that does not presuppose a need-satisfying function. Needless to say, the patient will not welcome any of this, and the therapist will need as much luck as skill to be successful. Nonetheless, if the therapist is able to produce tension and some regression in sessions and is able further to acknowledge and tolerate the patient's resulting distress, there is at least the possibility of a relationship not built on need satisfaction.

Having said all of this on the subject of not making the patient feel better, there are several things the therapist ought to do that will make the patient feel better. These, however, are designed to increase the patient's sense of personal competence, and this is different from communicating that the patient is weak and needy and therefore must be rescued from his or her upset. Any intervention that builds up the patient's ability to manage difficult situations and endure painful affect undermines affective lability and must therefore be used.

One such approach is to teach the patient deep relaxation techniques. There are several such techniques, and any will serve the therapist's purposes, depending on which ones the therapist knows. These include hypnosis, deep breathing, tai chi chuan, and the process of systematically tensing and relaxing muscle groups. The therapist introduces the subject by commenting on the patient's chronic difficulty managing tension and suggesting that there are ways to relieve such tension. These techniques should not be taught once or twice but must be taught many times, until the patient is comfortable with them and can achieve a state of deep relaxation relatively quickly. The more the patient practices these techniques, the more useful they will be. While initially an entire session will be needed to achieve a state of deep relaxation, with practice less time is needed. Eventually sessions can simply begin or end with such practice. The goal is to give the patient the competence to manage moods and feelings on his or her own. In itself this competence undermines the patient's sense of neediness.

There are times when therapists will be forced to intervene directly to help or rescue affectively labile patients. When therapists find a patient engaged in dangerous circumstances, they must act to protect the patient. It is my experience that such situations hold more promise of bringing treatment to a halt than furthering therapy, since these interventions usually create a crisis that is hard to resolve. Examples include learning that a patient is planning to run away, is using drugs heavily, or is engaged in a relationship that is physically dangerous.

It is possible that the patient will see the therapist as someone capable of recognizing his or her weaknesses and moving to offer protection. Theoretically this could help the patient see the therapist as a different kind of adult, one who can sort out what the patient can realistically be expected to face and master. It is, however, much more likely that the patient will be furious at the therapist's interference and will be unwilling to cooperate further. Even if the patient's anger can be resolved, there is always the danger that the patient will simply be renewed in the conviction that relationships are built on need and that the therapist has accepted the role of someone who meets the patient's needs.

The agenda I have outlined is exceptionally difficult to carry out on an outpatient basis, and it is much more likely that the treatment will fail than that it will succeed. I want to call attention again to my earlier statement that affectively labile patients are much better treated in a residential setting than in the therapist's private office or clinic.

RESIDENTIAL TREATMENT OF AFFECTIVELY LABILE ADOLESCENTS

The biggest obstacles in outpatient therapy with affectively labile patients are their dismal view of adults and their reluctance to bring their problems into the session. Both obstacles can be overcome in residential treatment, where a group process can be used, bypassing reliance on an adult authority, and where situations can be designed that will bring the patient face to face with problems. Indeed, in residential treatment with these patients, it is a mistake to use individual therapy until resistance is ended and the patient is committed to change. Treatment should center on peer interactions, which can be used to engineer situations the patient will find problematic.

Out-of-control patients—including affectively labile youth—typically show two traits: they have little use for adult authority, and they are highly reactive to peer pressure. Residential treatment can take advantage of these traits and turn them to treatment's advantage in ways that outpatient therapy cannot. Outpatient therapy is, after all, a matter of being in the hands of an adult authority, and there is no way to manage peer influence in the patient's life. There are many opportunities therefore for the therapist's influence to be lost completely. By contrast, residential treatment can revolve around group process, and staff can (and should) be trained to manage that process rather than treat patients directly. The goal of treatment should be to bring peer pressure to bear on each patient's pathology.

In the case of affectively labile patients, three general problem areas can be addressed in residential care that will encompass most of the dynamics described earlier in this chapter. Working through these problem areas will move patients past the resistance phase of treatment. First, there is the problem of separateness, or the affectively labile patient's allergy to individuation. Affectively labile patients will seek to avoid autonomous functioning, since any hint of autonomy would imply competence on their part and would therefore threaten them with abandonment and aloneness. Consequently, they can be expected to seek dependent relationships with peers, attaching themselves to one or more fellow patients in an attempt to deny any possibility of initiative or autonomy on their part. They can further be expected to minimize and avoid all conflict with favored peers, since tension implies difference, which in turn implies separateness. The resulting pattern is one of interpersonal weakness and neediness.

The second general problem area that must be addressed in order to take these patients past the resistance phase is their intolerance of painful affect. This is most likely to be evident in treatment by the patient's response to difficult and distressing issues and situations. Affectively labile patients cannot easily confront painful themes and issues, nor can they face confrontation and criticism by peers with any equanimity. Such situations force these patients to feel distress and to contain it, and this is something they cannot easily accomplish. Those working with these patients will have the chance to see their difficulty facing and managing pain whenever they are pressed to deal with the issues that led to treatment, when they are homesick, or when they are pressured by their peers. Affectively labile patients generally react to these situations by parading their weaknesses—by falling apart emotionally, threatening or attempting self-harm or self-mutilation, and rebuking others for not making them feel better.

These two general problem areas can be brought to the forefront of treatment by maneuvering patients into encounters that force them to behave competently in a situation that entails some tension with peers. Behaving competently will in itself produce painful affect, as these patients begin to feel anxiety over the possibility of losing the neediness necessary (as they see it) to maintain relatedness with others. If the situation they are forced to handle competently is built around conflict with one or more peers, they have the opportunity to learn that competence and conflict do not necessarily lead to loss of relatedness. The key to this part of treatment is forcing patients to endure and work through the upset they feel rather than give up and behave incompetently. They will almost certainly regress in such a predicament, a regression that must be contained and worked through so that the sequence can be repeated, probably several times.

In a residential program that uses group process competently, patients can usually be placed in encounters that leave them no options beyond some sort of conflict with others. Affectively labile patients will try hard to avoid the conflict or will enter into conflict only in order to give in masochistically, thereby hoping that the other will see their neediness and reconcile with them. Staff must be prepared to hold these patients' feet to the fire, forcing them over and over to collide with peers and preventing any easy submission and masochistic rapprochement. Some patients will engage in a lengthy and trying regression, hoping to make everyone else pay such a price that their incompetence and neediness will finally be accepted.

Sally was a 16-year-old whose history included a long series of relationships in which she was abused and taken advantage of by those she needed. She was roughed up and raped by boyfriends, although she typically tolerated such behavior from them as a way of proving that she truly loved and needed them. She used drugs heavily; even she was aware that her friends associated with her only because she would share her drugs with them. Sometimes she prostituted herself to obtain drugs for her friends in hopes they would like her more. She routinely had the experience of being used sexually and not receiving the drugs she was promised, and when she did obtain drugs her friends often stole them from her. These things finally did not matter to Sally, who would do anything to keep from being alone. Even though she was angry at the abuse she received, she put up with it.

In residential treatment Sally showed an almost complete inability to make anyone else unhappy. She could not bring herself to say or do anything that might conceivably upset one of her peers. She was docile and passive, letting herself be taken advantage of without protest. She could not bring herself to look at this behavior nor at similar behaviors prior to admission, and would become desperate and depressed if pressed.

The staff designed an intervention to force Sally to tolerate conflict with others and the inevitable pain this would carry. The patients always began each day with a full and thorough cleaning of the unit. Each peer was assigned a task, and the execution of the task was supervised by one peer who was given the role of chore boss for the week. Staff gave Sally this role, since it routinely led to conflict over who received the easier tasks and also on how well those tasks were carried out. After each day's cleaning, staff inspected the unit to judge how well the chores had been carried out, accepting the work if the cleaning had been done well or assigning some adverse consequence for the unit (such as doing the cleaning over again during free time that day) if they had not.

Sally could not force herself to make her peers do their jobs well and routinely approved poor work. This meant, of course, that the unit failed inspection each day. Sally was prepared to accept this. She hung her head, looked thoroughly miserable, and talked of her incompetence as chore boss. While Sally's peers were irritated, they eventually felt sorry for her and would encourage her to do better.

She would not do better the next day, however, since the pattern fit nicely into her pathology. She paraded her weakness and neediness for all to see.

Staff therefore made an important adjustment. They announced that Sally would keep the job of chore boss for a second week and that if the unit failed inspection everyone would receive an adverse consequence except for Sally, who would be rewarded. This intervention placed Sally in a bind: she would have conflict with her peers one way or the other, either through forcing them to do a better job or through winning a reward while they were punished. Upon hearing this, Sally collapsed emotionally, and chores had to be delayed nearly an hour while she wept and protested that this was unfair. Eventually chores were carried out, failed inspection as usual, and everyone except Sally was given extra work to do, while Sally was given extra dessert at lunch.

Sally's peers were unhappy with her and began to press her angrily to "get your act together" and "do your job right." Sally was unable therefore to win the illusion of closeness with her peers through being inept and then feeling badly about it. Her peers were the ones saying, in effect, that they would not accept her unless she behaved competently. By the end of that week and one additional week for good measure, Sally was managing the situation quite differently. She became an effective chore boss, learning to confront her peers on sloppy work and finding that doing this cemented relationships rather than ended them. While she had to face this issue in several other ways before her discharge many months later, this was the first progress she showed in what became a very successful treatment.

The third problem area to be addressed in residential treatment is the affectively labile patient's distorted time sense. As long as these patients experience time as a series of crises, they cannot manage any area of life more competently. If events quickly take on crisis proportions, the only thing on the patient's mind is getting rid of the intolerable tension, which usually means reaching closure as rapidly as possible. While a premature closure does in fact stop the crisis and its resulting tension, it solves nothing else and keeps the patient from learning the benefits of waiting, of taking time to see what happens and thereby learning that feelings tend to moderate with the passage of time.

At first glance it might seem that residential treatment should address the patient's distorted time sense through engaging the patient in a number of projects that are slow to unfold and require patience to complete. Of course, residential treatment should involve such projects; there is always virtue in activities that require time to accomplish, and whenever possible patients should have to wait for feedback, rewards, and closure. This does broaden the time sense and teaches patience. However, the strategy of making patients wait does not in itself alter the sense of crisis, which is built on the patient's sense that the world is not predictable and that relationships can be severed quickly. As long as relationships seem tenuous, time cannot be experienced as benevolent: whether it moves slowly or quickly, time will seem to be moving toward a dark future where abandonment is inevitable. The problem to be solved, then, is whether the future can seem promising or at least manageable, whether the patient can feel durable enough to master what happens.

It is the staff's manner of responding that eventually allows affectively labile patients to experience the passage of time as benign and, therefore, themselves as able to endure and adapt. In popular psychology, it is often thought that mental health professionals should go out of their way to be sympathetic, supportive, and encouraging with patients who seem weak, depressed, and needy. The idea behind this view is that such patients are lacking in self-esteem and that such esteem will be built up through encouraging, sympathetic responses. Unhappily, the result is likely to be the opposite of what is intended. When staff go out of their way to avoid criticism, pressure, or confrontation, patients learn that the staff see them as fragile and weak, and as long as they are treated in this way they will feel fragile and weak.

This is not to say that the opposite is necessarily any more desirable. There is no automatic virtue in being hard and abrasive. Such responses will not feel terribly different to affectively labile patients than what they drew from friends prior to treatment. They are used to drawing sadism from those around them, and they will see staff's sadism as something to which they must submit in order to display the weakness that will allow the relationship to continue. When working with affectively labile patients, staff should take pains neither to be sympathetic and supportive nor to be hard and abrasive. Neither approach communicates that the patient is (or can become) durable and that the future can be handled.

The proper approach is to be sensitive yet unmoved. Staff must show sensitivity by being able to appreciate what the affectively labile patient is struggling with and how difficult the patient's position is. Staff must communicate this by describing what they see as the patient's state of mind and acknowledging how hard matters are. However, they must never praise patients for work that is poor, minimize the extent of problems, or do anything else that is designed to make patients feel better. Such a style is far from sensitive; it communicates that the patient is viewed as weak and inept, someone who cannot handle the truth and of whom little is expected. This is not empathic but, rather, cements the patient's pathology. Consequently, staff must adopt a sensitive approach that allows them to empathize with the patient *without trying to make the patient feel better.*

Staff must therefore be unmoved by the patient's distress. While acknowledging what the patient is facing, they must nonetheless continue to speak the truth, telling the patient what needs to be done and why and insisting that the patient do it. Patients will almost certainly attempt a wide number of maneuvers designed to avoid the tasks placed before them. These may include self-harm, physical attacks on staff or peers, elopement attempts, oppositional behavior, hunger strikes, and attempts to create chaos on the unit. The key variable in how staff respond to these and other attempts to avoid moving forward is that staff must remain professional. This means that they must not take the patient's resistance personally nor grow angry at it. Rather, they must handle each situation calmly and confidently, communicating to the patient that they are not blown away or distressed. In any competent residential center there are clear policies and procedures for facing the problems patients can create, and staff must use these as their structure to negotiate the problems affectively labile patients cause. The aim is to behave predictably and competently in the face of the patient's distress.

When staff are able to remain sensitive yet unmoved, which is to say empathic and yet professional, they give an important message to the affectively labile patient that they recognize what is going on and yet do not see the situation as unmanageable. The staff's steady predictability in handling the crises the patient creates in turn gives a model for how the patient handles his or her own crises. Being able to work with staff who clearly know the patient and yet demand adaptive behavior communicates to the patient that relationships can be built on something other then neediness and that a durable self can be valued by others. Staff's steady and predictable responses make the world and the future seem more knowable, less tinged with risk.

FURTHER TREATMENT ISSUES

As mentioned earlier, affectively labile patients can be expected to regress whenever they make progress. It is as if they realize that they are moving away from the only basis for relatedness—neediness—and panic at the thought that they will surely bring about the abandonment they fear. Therapists should not only be prepared for the inevitable steps backward but should predict this to the patient. If the regression does not occur, this prediction does no harm, and if it does occur the therapist seems more knowing and trustworthy as a result. Progress with such patients is always a series of forwards and backwards movements. By remaining aware of this and preparing families for it, therapists counter the understandable discouragement that might otherwise be felt.

Finally, there is the question of medication. These patients usually show depressive symptoms, and antidepressant medication ought to be considered. In my experience, such medication seldom has a significant impact, oddly enough. Nonetheless, therapists are probably remiss if they do not refer patients for a medication evaluation. My sense is that such medication at best builds something of a floor under the patient's mood, preventing the lowest moods, but it is very unlikely to lead to significant strength or progress by itself. My experience further is that a low dose of antipsychotic medication is more likely to be useful, particularly during periods of crisis and regression (cf. Kroll 1988).

CONCLUSIONS

The affectively labile adolescent may come to treatment with the same symptoms as other out-of-control youths, but treatment carries several unusual features. To begin with, it is, I believe, harder to engage these patients in therapy than is the case with other out-of-control adolescents, with the possible exception of patients using the schizoid defense. It is so much harder that outpatient therapy is not the recommended form of treatment. In addition, therapists may find that they are not facing a form of resistance so much as a personality style that is in the process of crystallizing. These youths seem to me to be organizing along borderline themes and issues, although I do not believe it is possible to approach them in therapy in the same ways we would approach adult borderline patients.

Moving these patients beyond affective lability is largely contingent on being able to correct their distorted time sense, preparing them to endure apparent crises and learn that these tend to resolve themselves without unwise, frequently degrading, and masochistic responses. In turn this ability to endure goes hand in hand with discovering that lasting attachments are not built on neediness and weakness.

REFERENCES

Aarons, A. (1970). Normality and abnormality in adolescence. *Psycho-analytic Study of the Child* 25:309–339. New Haven, CT: Yale University Press.

Aichhorn, A. (1964). *Delinquency and Child Guidance—Selected Papers*. New York: International Universities Press.

Bach, S. (1985). *Narcissistic States and the Therapeutic Process*. New York: Jason Aronson.

Berliner, B. (1940). Libido and reality in masochism. *Psychoanalytic Quarterly* 9:2–333.

Biederman, J. (1997). Is there a childhood form of bipolar disorder? *Harvard Mental Health Letter*, March, p. 8.

Blos, P. (1983). The contributions of psychoanalysis to the psychotherapy of adolescents. *Psychoanalytic Study of the Child* 38:577–600. New Haven, CT: Yale University Press.

Breuer, J., and Freud, S. (1895). Studies in hysteria. *Standard Edition* 2.

Burgner, M., and Edgcumbe, R. (1972). Some problems in the conceptualization of early object relationships. Part II: The concept of object constancy. *Psychoanalytic Study of the Child* 27:315–333. New Haven, CT: Yale University Press.

Cameron, N. (1963). *Personality Development and Psychopathology: A Dynamic Approach*. Boston: Houghton-Mifflin.

Chasseguet-Smirgel, J. (1984). *Creativity and Perversion*. New York: Norton.

—— (1985).*The Ego Ideal: A Psychoanalytic Essay on the Malady of the Ideal*, trans. P. Barrows. New York: Norton.

Chessick, R. (1977). *Intensive Psychotherapy of the Borderline Patient*. New York: Jason Aronson.

Cohen, C. (1969). Psychotherapy: the situation and its participants. Unpublished manuscript. Copies available from the author of this book.

Cohen, C., and Sherwood, V. (1991). *Becoming a Constant Object in Psychotherapy with the Borderline Patient*. Northvale, NJ: Jason Aronson.

Deutsch, H. (1944). *The Psychology of Women*. New York: Grune & Stratton.

Dickes, R. (1967). Severe therapeutic disruptions of the therapeutic alliance. *Journal of the American Psychoanalytic Association* 15:508–534.

—— (1975). Technical considerations of the therapeutic and working alliances. *International Journal of Psychoanalytic Psychology* 4:1–24.

Eissler, K. R. (1950). Ego-psychological implications of the psychoanalytic treatment of delinquents. *Psychoanalytic Study of the Child* 5:97–121. New York: International Universities Press.

—— (1958). Notes on problems of technique in the psychoanalytic treatment of adolescents: With some remarks on perversion. *Psychoanalytic Study of the Child* 13:223–254. New York: International Universities Press.

Evans, R. (1976). Development of the treatment alliance in the analysis of an adolescent boy. *Psychoanalytic Study of the Child* 31:193–224. New Haven, CT: Yale University Press.

Fairbairn, W. R. D. (1952). *An Object Relations Theory of the Personality*. New York: Basic Books.

Ferenczi, S. (1936). Male and female: psychoanalytic reflections on the "theory of genitality" and on secondary and tertiary sex differences. *Psychoanalytic Quarterly* 5:249–260.

Fisch, R., Weakland, J., and Segal, L. (1982). *The Tactics of Change: Doing Therapy Briefly*. San Francisco: Jossey-Bass.

Fraiberg, S. (1955). Some considerations in the introduction to therapy in puberty. *Psychoanalytic Study of the Child* 10:264–286. New York: International Universities Press.

Freud, A. (1952). The mutual influence in the development of ego and id. Introduction to the discussion.*Psychoanalytic Study of the Child* 7:42–50. New York: International Universities Press.

———— (1958). Adolescence. *Psychoanalytic Study of the Child* 13:255–278. New York: International Universities Press.

———— (1965). *Normality and Pathology in Childhood: Assessments of Development.* New York: International Universities Press.

Freud, S. (1912a). The dynamics of transference. *Standard Edition* 12:97–108.

———— (1912b). Totem and taboo. *Standard Edition* 13:1–161.

———— (1914). On narcissism: an introduction. *Standard Edition* 14:73–104.

———— (1920). Beyond the pleasure principle. *Standard Edition* 18:7–64.

———— (1923). The ego and the id. *Standard Edition* 19:12–66.

———— (1924). The dissolution of the Oedipus Complex. *Standard Edition* 19:173–179.

———— (1926). Inhibitions, symptoms, and anxiety. *Standard Edition* 20:77–178.

———— (1940). An outline of psychoanalysis. *Standard Edition* 23:144–207.

Friedman, L. (1988). *The Anatomy of Psychotherapy.* Hillsdale, NJ: Analytic Press.

Geleerd, E. (1957). Some aspects of psychoanalytic treatment of adolescents. *Psychoanalytic Study of the Child* 12:263–283. New York: International Universities Press.

Giovacchini, P. (1979). *Treatment of Primitive Mental States.* New York: Jason Aronson.

Gitelson, M. (1948). Character synthesis: the psychotherapeutic problem in adolescence.*American Journal of Orthopsychiatry* 18:63–86.

Goldberg, C. (1973). *The Human Circle—An Existential Approach to the New Group Therapies.* Chicago: Nelson-Hall.

Greenson, R. (1967). *The Technique and Practice of Psychoanalysis,* vol. I. New York: International Universities Press.

Grunberger, B. (1989). *New Essays on Narcissism,* trans. D. Macey. London: Free Association Books.

Guntrip, H. S. (1969). *Schizoid Phenomena, Object Relations, and the Self.* New York: International Universities Press.

———— (1971). *Psychoanalytic Theory, Therapy, and the Self.* New York: Basic Books.

Haley, J. (1963). *Strategies of Psychotherapy*. New York: Grune & Stratton.
———— (1986). *The Power Tactics of Jesus Christ and Other Essays*. New York: Norton.
Harley, M. (1970). On some problems of technique in the analysis of early adolescents. *Psychoanalytic Study of the Child* 25:99–121. New York: International Universities Press.
Hinshaw, S. (1987). On the distinction between attention deficits/hyperactivity and conduct problems/aggression in child psychopathology. *Psychological Bulletin* 101:443–463.
Jacobson, E. (1961). Adolescent moods and the remodeling of psychic structure in adolescence. *Psychoanalytic Study of the Child* 16:164–183. New York: International Universities Press.
Joseph, R. (1982). The neuropsychology of development: hemispheric laterality, limbic language and the origin of thought. *Journal of Clinical Psychology* 38:4–33.
Kaiser, H. (1965). *Effective Psychotherapy: The Contribution of Hellmuth Kaiser*, ed. Louis B. Fierman. New York: Free Press.
Katan, A. (1935). From the analysis of a bed wetter. *Psychoanalytic Quarterly* 4:50–61.
Kernberg, O. (1975). *Borderline Conditions and Pathological Narcissism*. New York: Jason Aronson.
Kierkegaard, S. (1846/1992). *Concluding Unscientific Postscript to Philosophical Fragments*, vol. I, trans. H. V. Hong and E. H. Hong. Princeton, NJ: Princeton University Press.
Kohut, H. (1971). *The Analysis of the Self: A Systematic Approach to the Psychoanalytic Treatment of Narcissistic Personality Disorders*. New York: International Universities Press.
Kroll, J. (1988). *The Challenge of the Borderline Patient: Competency in Diagnosis and Treatment*. New York: Norton.
Laing, R. D. (1960). *The Divided Self*. London: Tavistock.
Laing, R. D., and Esterson, A. (1964). *Sanity, Madness, and the Family*. New York: Basic Books.
Lampl-De Groot, J. (1960). On adolescence. *Psychoanalytic Study of the Child* 15:95–103. New York: International Universities Press.
Langs, R. (1974a). *The Technique of Psychoanalytic Psychotherapy, Volume 1*. New York: Jason Aronson.

———— (1974b). *The Technique of Psychoanalytic Psychotherapy, Volume 2*. New York: Jason Aronson.

Leary, T. (1957). *Interpersonal Diagnosis of Personality: A Functional Theory and Methodology for Personality Evaluation*. New York: Ronald Press.

Mahler, M., Pine, F., and Bergman, A. (1975). *The Psychological Birth of the Human Infant*. New York: Basic Books.

Marohn, R. (1977). The "juvenile impostor": some thoughts of narcissism and the delinquent. In *Adolescent Psychiatry: Developmental and Clinical Studies*, vol. V, ed. S. Feinstein and P. Giovacchini, pp. 186–212. New York: Jason Aronson.

Masterson, J. (1972). *Treatment of the Borderline Adolescent: A Developmental Approach*. New York: Wiley.

———— (with Costello, J.) (1980). *From Borderline Adolescent to Functioning Adult: The Test of Time*. New York: Brunner/Mazel.

———— (1981). *Narcissistic and Borderline Disorders: An Integrated Developmental Approach*. New York: Brunner/Mazel.

McDougall, J. (1972). Primal scene and sexual perversion. *International Journal of Psycho-Analysis* 5:371–384.

McElroy, S., Strakowski, S., West, S., et al. (1997). Phenomenology of adolescent and adult mania in hospitalized patients with bipolar disorder. *American Journal of Psychiatry* 154:44–48.

Menaker, E. (1979). *Masochism and the Emergent Ego: Selected Papers of Esther Menaker*, ed. L. Lerner. New York: Human Sciences Press.

Miller, D. (1986). *Attack on the Self: Adolescent Behavior Disturbances and Their Treatment*. Northvale, NJ: Jason Aronson.

Miller, L. (1988). Neuropsychological perspectives on delinquency. *Behavioral Sciences and the Law* 6:409–428.

Modell, A. (1984). *Psychoanalysis in a New Context*. New York: International Universities Press.

Noshpitz, J. (1957). Opening phase in the psychotherapy of adolescents with character disorders. *Bulletin of the Menninger Clinic* 21:153–164.

Nunberg, H. (1926). The will to recovery. In *Practice and Theory of Psychoanalysis*, vol. I, pp. 75–88. New York: International Universities Press.

Ogden, T. (1982). *Projective Identification and Psychotherapeutic Technique*. New York: Jason Aronson.

Reich, A. (1940/1973). A contribution to the psychoanalysis of extreme submissiveness in women. In *Annie Reich: Psychoanalytic Contributions*. New York: International Universities Press.

Rinsley, D. (1980). *Treatment of the Severely Disturbed Adolescent*. New York: Jason Aronson.

———— (1982). *Borderline and Other Self Disorders*. New York: Jason Aronson.

Sartre, J. (1956). *Being and Nothingness*, trans. H. Barnes. New York: Pocket Books.

Segal, H. (1964). *Introduction to the Work of Melanie Klein*. New York: Basic Books.

Shapiro, D. (1965). *Neurotic Styles*. New York: Basic Books.

Shapiro, S., and Garfinkel, B. (1986). The occurrence of behavior disorders in children. *Journal of the American Academy of Child Psychiatry* 25: 809–819.

Sherwood, V. (1987). The schizoid personality in light of Camus's actor. *Bulletin of the Menninger Clinic* 51:158–169.

———— (1990). The first stage of treatment with the conduct disordered adolescent: overcoming Narcissistic Resistance. *Psychotherapy* 27:380–387.

Sherwood, V., and Cohen, C. (1994). *Psychotherapy of the Quiet Borderline Patient: The As-If Personality Revisited*. Northvale, NJ: Jason Aronson.

Spiegel, L. (1951). A psychoanalytic theory of adolescence. *Psychoanalytic Study of the Child* 6:111–132. New York: International Universities Press.

Sprince, M. (1971). An adolescent boy's battle against recovery. *Psychoanalytic Study of the Child* 26:453–483. New Haven, CT: Yale University Press.

Stabenau, J. (1984). Implications of family history of alcoholism, antisocial personality and sex differences in alcohol dependence. *American Journal of Psychiatry* 41:1178–1182.

Sullivan, H. (1956). *Clinical Studies in Psychiatry*. New York: Norton.

Watzlawick, P., Weakland, J., and Fisch, R. (1974). *Change: Principles of Problem Formation and Problem Resolution*. New York: Norton.

Willock, B. (1986). Narcissistic vulnerability in the hyperaggressive child: the disregarded (unloved, uncared-for) self. *Psychoanalytic Psychology* 3:59–80.

———— (1987). The devalued (unloved, repugnant) self—a second facet of narcissistic vulnerability in the aggressive, conduct disordered child. *Psychoanalytic Psychology* 4:219–240.

Winnicott, D. W. (1960/1965). Ego distortion in terms of true and false self. In *The Maturational Processes and the Facilitating Environment*, pp.140–152. New York: International Universities Press, 1965.

INDEX

Bodies, and schizoid defense,
    157–159, 167–170
Borderline pathology
    and affectively labile adolescents,
        183, 188–189
    similarity of schizoid defense to, 147
Boredom
    and schizoid adolescents, 149, 170–
        171
    and sense of disconnected time, 80–
        81
Breuer, J., 33
Burgner, M., 181

Cameron, N., 84
Cause-and-effect sequences, 80
    acceptance of, 55–56
    in narcissistic resistance, 75–76, 80
Chasseguet-Smirgel, J.
    on drive for development, 69–70
    on oedipal struggle, 56
    on role of ego ideal, 54
Chessick, R., 60
Cohen, C.
    on false self system, 153
    on identity and patterns of
        resistance, 27
    on schizoid self-consciousness,
        155–156
    on therapy with adolescents, 10,
        171
    on violating patient's expectations, 11
Commitments, and identity, 27
Competence
    and choppy time sense, 80
    increasing in treatment, 193, 196–
        198
    lack of, 25, 130–131, 176
    questioning by prescribing
        symptoms, 136
    risks of, 183–184, 188
    and sense of accomplishment, 77

Compliance
    episodic, 78–79
    in false self system, 153
    to therapist, 85
Conduct Disorder diagnosis, 2
Conflict, avoidance of, 195–198
Confrontations, to counter narcissistic
    resistance, 74–75, 79
Contempt. *See also* Adults, disdain for
    as response to masochists, 106–
        107
    for therapist, 14–15
Control
    adolescent striving for, 38, 42,
        159
    and affectively labile adolescents,
        177–178, 200–201
    regaining through prescribing
        symptoms, 140–141
Cooperation, and therapeutic alliance,
    33–35
Countertransference
    with masochistic patients, 100
    in reaction to adolescent patients,
        10
Crimes. *See* Delinquency
Cryptic comments, to defeat paranoid
    resistance, 145

Defenses, 160. *See also* Schizoid
    defense
    false self system as, 153
    masochism as, 109–110
    passivity as, 154
    resistance as ego strength, 38
Defiance, 85
    of children of sadistic fathers,
        65–66
    of paranoid adolescents, 21, 123–
        126
    reframing masochism as, 118–120
    using in treatment, 46–47, 134